GEORGE CAPPANNELLI

Conversations with Merlin

Lessons on Life, Leadership and Noble Governance From The Wizsard Who Mentored The Future King

"*There lies before us, if we choose,*
continual progress in happiness,
knowledge, and wisdom, but we must appeal
to human beings, remember our humanity,
and forget the rest. If we do so,
the way lies open to a new Paradise."
Albert Einstein

Contents

Foreword

"To be shaken out of the ruts of ordinary perception,
To be shown for a few timeless hours the other and inner worlds,
Not as they appear to (one) obsessed with words and notions.
But as they are apprehended, directly and unconditionally,
By (our souls) – this is an experience of inestimable value."

- Aldous Huxley

Preface

Seniors become the midwives of souls, the evoctateurs of self and society."

Jean Houston on Do Not Go Quietly

"I personally found [Say Yes to Change] to be provocative and practical. I am going through a period of change in my career and found the exercises to be easy and logical. ... Say Yes to Change is refreshing, powerful, and unique. Much is made about the new world that we live in, but few other books offer advice on the way we can personally navigate through these uncharted waters. This book provides us with that road map and allows you to go wherever your true desires direct us. I highly recommend it as required reading for everyone, young and old."

–Cody Plott, former COO of Pebble Beach Resort, President and CEO of Colliers Seeley

"Millions of Cultural Creatives are both changing their lives and creating a new culture in response to the crises of our age. H you are one of those millions, you know how important it is to balance your Inner Work and your work in the world. This book offers a wise, no-frills, practical way to do your Inner Work. Try this book-you need it."

–Paul H. Ray, Ph.D., coauthor of The Cultural Creatives: How 50 Million People Are
Changing the World

"In Do Not Go Quietly, the Cappannellis remind us that the road to a more conscious future passes directly through the process of harvesting the wisdom and experience of our past and participating individually and collectively in writing a new 'third act' for the future."

Rabbi Zalman Schachter-Shalomi, author of *Age-ing To Sage-ing* and the father of
spiritual eldering

"**George Cappannelli** helped us meet our current and future workload by creating a new operating state that improves trust and teamwork and propels our vision."

-General Donald Cromer, President, Hughes Space & Communications

"Suffice it to say you are a master of your craft."

-Cor Westerhoff, director of Government Programs, Space Systems/Loral

"I found Say Yes to Change to be a powerful and insightful book. It offers the reader practical and helpful tools on how to face life's challenges with confidence. A necessary read for all who wish to realize their full potential."

-Catherine Cardinal, Ph.D., author of The Ten Commandments of Self-Esteem and The

Ten Commandments of Relationships

"The Cappannellis remind us that our fear of change, like our fear of so many things, blocks our ability to experience and express love, which is our natural inheritance. Their practical insights open the door for the reader to experience change as a positive experience leading to oneness."

-Gerald G. Jampolsky, M.D., author of Forgiveness: The Greatest Healer of All

"Authenticity is a terrific book for our times! George and Sedena Cappannelli are 'truth-tellers who have written a gem of a book. I recommend it to faith-based people everywhere."

The Very Reverend Edward H Harrison, Dean of St John's Cathedral

"George and Sedena have written a thoughtful, thorough, and surprising book on the wisdom of aging. Do Not Go Quietly inspires and encourages us to live fully at any age; to act boldly for the sake of the world as well as for our souls."

Michael Meade, Noted Mythologist, Poet, and Story Teller

"George Cappannelli's work exposed me to more concise, contemporary improvement skills than I have ever seen presented in one place at one time."

-Boyd Willat, founder of Day Runner, President of SENSA Pens, and Willat Writing

Instruments

"I am awed by your ability and desire to impact lives. What a career to have!"

-Rhodes Robinson, founder of Environmental Service, Inc.

"Purpose and meaning, very important subjects, are explored in voices that have been there and know the ground. The Cappannellis are the real deal. Their coaching work with world-class organizations and high-performing individuals gets to the heart of the matter and, in the end, it is certainly the heart that matters when dealing with the subject of meaning and purpose."

Melina Borrows, Contributing Writer at Cosmopolitan & Ladies' Home Journal

"During the last fifteen years and especially during my tenure as director of Human Resources for the International Division, I have used a wide range of consulting and training services, but none have been more impactful than George Cappannelli's work."

-Jerry LoPorto, GIA Personnel Manager, Digital/Compaq

"As a result of George Cappannelli's work, people are working just as hard, but now there is trust, mutual support, openness, and sensitivity. It's a different place."

-Jeanne Scott, director of Corporate Training, Taco Bell

"Do No Go Quietly offers invaluable insights into what is an increasingly vital subject of our time and our collective future. In its pages, you hear George and Sedena Cappannelli illuminate the Wisdom and life-affirming contributions about individuals who are −as I like to call it − moving from aging to saging."

Reverend Michael Bernard Beckwith

I

Part One

Chapter One - In The Beginning

He who has great power should use it lightly.
Seneca

Without being aware of it at the time, I began writing this book several decades ago. I was in my early thirties and struggling with issues of life purpose and meaning that many young men – and all human beings, if they are wise - periodically revisit.

As part of my search, I began working with a therapist who was affiliated with the C.G. Jung Institute in New York. Early in our relationship, he introduced me to something called The Active Imagination Process. It was an introduction that not only proved to be a very valuable gift at that time, but it has also brought me many other valuable benefits ever since. And not the least of these is this book.

My therapist told me Carl Jung had developed the process and that it had been refined and enriched by two of his former patients who had become close colleagues and collaborators. Barbara Hannah's book *"Encounters with the Soul"* would prove to be an invaluable, practical guide for me in experimenting with the Active Imagination Process, *and* Marie-Louise von Franz's work with fairy tales, myths, and alchemy brought me a host of equally valuable gifts.

As a result, during the time I worked with my therapist and periodically over the intervening years, I have utilized the Active Imagination Process, and recommend it highly to anyone who is committed to learning more about themselves and leading lives of greater meaning and purpose.

During those early years, I also discovered that a group of notable individuals, including Jacob Bohme, Emanuel Swedenborg, Samuel Coleridge, Ralph Waldo Emerson, Rudolf Steiner, Henry Corbin, Andrew Carnegie, James Hillman, and others, had experimented with different versions of this and similar processes and reported significant results.

Carnegie, for example, the 19th-century Scottish American self-made steel tycoon and philanthropist, reported that he used his version of this process to convene highly credentialed advisory boards that included major historical figures he greatly admired. Carnegie, I learned, even attributed his creation of the Steel Industry to information he received during one of these board meetings.

As a result, after months of experimenting with Jung's version of The Active Imagination process which was described as *"a meditation technique wherein the contents of one's unconscious are translated into images, narrative or personified as separate entities,"* I was inspired and intrigued enough by the gains Carnegie had reported in his dialogues with historical figures, to combine his technique with Jung's

This combination led me to begin a series of conversations with a historical figure who had fascinated me from the time I was first introduced to him as a young boy through stories about King Arthur and the Round Table. That figure, as is clear from the title of this book, is Merlin, wise man, scholar, magician, prophet, bard, and mystic. And it is my conversations with him that serve as the primary foundation for this book.

A Little More About Merlin

Before I tell you more about this book and my experience with these valuable dialogue techniques, I thought, in the interest of full disclosure, I would acknowledge that some hold several different perspectives on Merlin ranging from those who dispute his existence to those, like me, who have been inspired and enriched by him and consider him as important, and in some ways more so than many other figures who are described in the pages of history.

In the case of individuals who dispute Merlin's existence, I have found they also tend to dispute the existence of King Arthur, the Round Table, Camelot, and, indeed, many other inspiring individuals and uplifting events that have added meaning and a sense of magic and mystery to the historical record.

I cannot, of course, say for certain why these individuals hold so tenaciously to their denials; however, I do believe the quote by Aldous Huxley that begins this book provides us with a clue, as is clear from this excerpt:

> *"To be shaken out of the ruts of ordinary perception,*
> *To be shown for a few timeless hours the other and inner worlds,*
> *Not as they appear to be (one) obsessed with words and notions,*
> *But as they are apprehended, directly and unconditionally,*
> *By (our souls) – this is an experience of inestimable value."*

"Obsessed with words and notions." That has certainly been true for me more times than I care to admit. And based on the state of the world, it seems to also be true for many others who are currently navigating journeys on this physical plane at this very turbulent time in history. Especially, when it appears that many of us have turned away from the essential values, practices, and benefits advanced by the Wisdom Traditions and towards rationalism, materialism, and consumerism as our creeds.

I find this as sad as it is limiting. Indeed, I believe it is another clear sign that we are living in what Mythologist Michael Meade calls *The Age of the Great Forgetting,* a period in which there is a growing distance from the guidance of the Wisdom Traditions and a preoccupation with all things tangible, as well as an obsession with the worship of the God of Economics and the errant pursuit of security and safety which Helen Keller called *"A superstition that does not occur in nature, nor do the children of man, as a whole, experience it. Avoiding danger is not safer in the long run than outright exposure. Life is either a daring adventure or nothing."*

Indeed, for many of us, life seems to have become a mind-focused and rather humorless affair. We have replaced imagination, intuition, creativity, and that 'daring adventure' Keller spoke about with what Jung referred to as "believing" rather than "knowing." Yes, the vast majority of us in this digital/information age no longer honor what Merlin referred to often in our conversations as the Great Mystery and the integrity and honor of the quest. Instead, in the contemporary world, many of us now mimic the Apostle Thomas, also known as Doubting Thomas, and as a result, declare as real only what our five senses appear to verify.

This is especially true for those of us who, unfortunately, have been educated under what Brazilian educator Paulo Freire has called, The Pedagogy of the Oppressed. As well as the large number of us who have also, in the words of contemporary writer/shaman Don Miguel Ruiz, been domesticated.

So, some of us, at least some of the time, and others of us a lot of the time, tend to accept as true only that which is reported in the news and what is called the historical record. Which, upon reflection, seems an odd thing, since the vast majority of us know from our own experience in capturing and retelling our personal histories that, depending on the circumstances and the perceived consequences, we often tend to apply differing degrees of selective memory in this recounting.

Yes, our retelling often obscures some events, exaggerates others, and minimizes the recounting of those actions we believe do not present us in a favorable light. Indeed, in many instances, our retelling is like the versions of history that have been sanitized and altered by countless numbers of monarchs and rulers, and religious and military leaders in the past. And today, this sanitizing and editing is being done in plain sight by the Deceiver In Chief and the lackeys in his administration, whose goal is to advance Autocracy, Kleptocracy, and Theocracy as forms of governance that grant control to the few over the many.

These highly censored and manipulated versions of the historical record also generally leave out or try to minimize a host of misdeeds, misdemeanors, and, in many cases, major cruelties and crimes; things that they do not want those they control, and those who will come after them, to know about. Something that Donald Trump, the Deceiver in Chief, and his enablers are currently doing. Hoping, one can only assume, that those who come after them will accept their version of events and dismiss everything else as false and untrue.

There is a third group that advances a different perspective on Merlin. This group includes many authors and historians from Catholic Cleric Geoffrey of Monmouth (1095 to 1155) who it is believed used a combination of several historical figures to create Merlin, to contemporary Medieval Historian, Anne Lawrence-Mather who, in her True History of Merlin The Magician, described Merlin as *"a learned figure on the cutting edge of Medieval science and adapt in astrology, cosmology, prophecy, and natural magic who helped to put British history in world history."* She and others also claim that Merlin served as the tutor and advisor to Arthur before he became king and until Merlin was bewitched and imprisoned by Vivian, one of his apprentices, who is also thought to be the Lady of the Lake.

I share this information with you because, depending on your beliefs on the nature of reality and your experience with Huxley's "ruts of ordinary perception," you may be inclined to question or even dismiss the possibility that I conducted conversations with an individual from a previous historical period.

I am confident, however, that if you take even a little time to experiment with the Active Imagination Process, you will, at the very least, be surprised by the results. And if you are willing to go further and also experiment more deeply with meditation and prayer, with the use of some of plant-based medicines passed down to us from the ancients that support us in experiencing altered states of reality, as well as with some of the breathing techniques encouraged in yoga, Holotropic Breath Work and re birthing, if you spend time exploring the new scientific literature that now confirms the convergence of science and spirituality; and finally, if you are willing to temporarily suspend some of your biases and judgments while you read these words and concepts Merlin shared with me, I believe you will find that it is easier than you think to pierce the veil and experience a variety of inner and outer parallel worlds – worlds some scientists and refer to as "the non-local or the Imaginal Realm." And if you do just some of these things, I am confident your concept of reality will change and these other states of consciousness will soon become at least as influential, if not more so, than what you currently call 'reality.'

A Deeper Look at The Active Imagination Process

According to Carl Jung, Active Imagination can *"serve as a bridge between the conscious 'ego' and the unconscious and includes working with dreams and the creative self via imagination or fantasy. "*

"Jung linked active imagination with the processes of alchemy in that both - *"strive for oneness and interrelatedness from a set of fragmented and dissociated parts."*

Indeed, it has been said that while Jung's contributions to the practice and science of psychology are of tremendous value, his exploration of Active Imagination may end up being one of his most significant contributions to the field of human experience.

Jung found that Active Imagination could be explored through visualization, which has been described as a form of shamanic journeying, and this is how he used it. He also suggested, however, that *"Active Imagination can be practiced through automatic writing, or artistic activities such as dance, music, painting, sculpting, ceramics, crafts, etc.*

In Jung's experience, *"the patient can make himself creatively independent through this method, and that by painting himself (and you can substitute any or all of the creative practices listed above), he gives shape to himself. Active Imagination then permits the thought-forms of the unconscious, or inner self, and of the totality of the psyche, to act out whatever messages they are trying to communicate to the conscious mind."*

As I said earlier, I also learned about the practical use of Active Imagination through Barbara Hannah's book Encounters with the Soul, and from Marie-Louise von Franz's writings, I learned that Active Imagination was similar to the Alchemical process known as "Imaginata," a form of "conscious dreaming.".

Additional investigation disclosed that Theosophists from Jakob Bohme to Emanuel Swedenborg used a similar process they called 'imaginal cognition.' *"They believed it served as an 'organ of the soul, thanks to which humanity can establish a cognitive and vision relationship with an intermediate world."*

Samuel Taylor Coleridge, British poet and good friend of William Wordsworth, *"distinguished imagination, which expresses realities of an imaginal realm transcending any personal existence, from 'fancy, or fantasy, which expresses the creativity of the artistic soul."* In his words, *"imagination is the condition for cognitive participation in a sacramental universe."*

C.S. Lewis suggested that *"reason is the organ of truth, but imagination is the organ of meaning".*

Ralph Waldo Emerson said, *"When it is dark enough, you can see the stars."*-

To paraphrase Albert Einstein, *"Reason can take you from A to B, but imagination can take you everywhere."* And indeed, his imagination that allowed him to visualize riding a beam of light through the universe ultimately led to his articulation of the Theory of Relativity.

Although some, including Jung himself, warned that *"one should embark upon this process with due care and attentiveness,"* Jung also said that *"this technique had the potential not only to allow communication between the conscious and unconscious aspects of the personal psyche with its various components and inter-dynamics, but also between the personal and collective unconscious."*

James Hillman and Sonu Shamdasani suggested that *"active imagination in Jung's usage was an exposition of the unvoiced influences of the collective unconscious, shedding the terminology of psychology to work directly through mythic images."*

Rudolf Steiner suggested that *"imaginal cognition was an initial step on a path leading from rational consciousness toward ever-deeper spiritual experience."*

And Henry Corbin, philosopher, theologian, and Iranologist, considered imaginal cognition to be a *"purely spiritual faculty independent of the physical organism and thus surviving it."* He termed imagination, which transcends fantasy, as *"imaginatio vera."*

Corbin also suggested that by *"developing our imaginal perception, we can go beyond mere symbolic representations of archetypes to the point where new senses perceive directly the order of [supersensible] reality"*. To accomplish this passage from symbol to reality requires a *"transmutation of the being and the spirit."* He also considered the imaginal realm to be *"identical with the realm of angels described in many religions, which manifests not only through imagination but also in people's vocation and destiny."*

My Early Experiments With Active Imagination

What especially intrigued me about the Active Imagination Process was Jung's assertion that neurosis is *"a psychological crisis due to a state of disunity with oneself"* and that this crisis is something that can be welcomed, and not just treated as a dysfunction. In many ways, this one statement changed not only my receptivity to experimenting with Jungian psychology and therapy, but also the way I came to look at life in general.

In fact, instead of continuing to be confined by some of the limited beliefs and what I came to understand were little more than misconceptions and superstitions that I had been introduced to as a boy and had innocently accepted, I began to view my life as a journey of adventure and discovery and the world as school in which to explore, experiment, learn, and awaken up to new levels of consciousness.

I also learned that according to Jung, *"an outbreak of neurosis is purposeful, an opportunity to become conscious of who we are as opposed to who we think we are. And therefore, by working through the symptoms that invariably accompany neurosis − anxiety, fear, depression, guilt, shame, and particularly conflict, we can become aware of our limitations and discover our true strengths."*

This awareness also helped me to accept that my 'symptoms' were not personal flaws or dysfunctions that I had to live with − like some version of "original sin", but instead, they were individual entities or characters that inhabited my consciousness, and were, when I worked with them, temporary companions and allies. Through my use of the Active Imagination Process, I also had a direct experience of the role these 'entities' and 'disturbances' played in my life. And when I was true to it, this process helped me to better understand what Jung called 'individuation,' and what others in various spiritual and religious traditions call 'enlightenment.

My Choice

Since I was more comfortable with the written word than I was with other forms of artistic expression that would later play an important role in my life, I chose the word as the path I would take. And following the guidance of my therapist and using Barbara Hannah' book as an additional resource, I began writing down my dialogues with these different 'symptoms' as if I was writing a play with various characters, In my case, of course, the play was my life and the characters were the emotions/symptoms of anger, anxiety, fear, depression, guilt, sadness, etc. that came up at various times and often brought with them varying degrees of confusion and challenge.

Through doing this, I verified something else Barbara Hannah addressed. Although I might begin one of my dialogues with one 'symptom' - anger, for example - at some point in the conversation, this 'symptom' or character would often be replaced by another, and I would find myself talking to sadness or fear or guilt. While it would sometimes take me a little time to realize that this transition had occurred, eventually I would notice that there was a difference in the vocabulary being used by the new symptom I was conversing with. Sometimes I would recognize this change because there was a different feeling tone, rhythm, or syntax that would clue me in to the fact that a shift had occurred.

In this way, I was able to confirm something else Hannah had reported. She said, "*that our habitual responses in many life situations and interactions with other people generally mask deeper and more challenging 'symptoms' that we are not as comfortable with and therefore tend to avoid.*" This information allowed me to better understand why my default reaction in many circumstances was anger. Yes, I was more comfortable with anger than with sadness or despair, which were more challenging to admit and brought up deeper feelings of vulnerability.

Taking the lead from my therapist, I also found it very helpful to begin each dialogue with a question that asked permission of the 'symptoms' to engage with them. I found that this also helped me to not only honor the process, but to treat it as seriously as I did other conversations with people in my life whom I truly valued.

So I made it my practice to ask questions like - "Anger, can we have a conversation?" Or "Sadness, will you talk to me about what just happened?" At other times, I would ask the symptom – *"What are you trying to tell me?"* or *"What do you want me to know?"* These questions not only gave the dialogue process a much greater sense of reality, but it led me naturally to other questions and answers, and so on. And, as I said, I would record both my questions and the answers I received from the 'symptom(s).'

As you can imagine, there were plenty of times, especially early in my experiments with Active Imagination, that the process felt awkward and forced. And as a result, I would find myself questioning whether I was actually talking to a 'symptom' and getting legitimate answers or just 'making stuff up.' In fact, on more than a few occasions, I would close the notebook and dismiss the process as foolish and a waste of time. Thanks to my therapist's encouragement, however, and my deep respect for Jung and his work, I kept experimenting and eventually began to experience some very real benefits.

I also began to notice other things as well. The answers I received to the questions I asked brought me valuable information and useful insights. And these insights and information were often not things I had previously considered, and in some instances, they were things that I did not even fully understand until some time had passed and I had gained a better perspective on their validity. I also began to notice that many of the answers I recorded contained a level of genuine common sense that I could not refute, even when I did not like or want to admit a truth they disclosed about myself or one of my actions. And finally, the information I received gave me insights and clues regarding specific things I needed to work on or skills I needed to develop.

As my experimentation with the process continued, I also acknowledged that the answers were not originating from what I recognized as my usual inner voice, but instead from a deeper, more profound source of wisdom that had previously been beyond my reach.

Taken together, these experiences confirmed the fact that I was participating in an actual dialogue or conversation with a real 'symptom' or character that allowed me to experience a more authentic understanding of my motives, greater awareness of some of my unhealed wounds, and more honest admissions of my needs, vulnerabilities, and desires.

Consequently, I filled several notebooks with these dialogues and found myself feeling very grateful for what I can only describe as the wisdom I received and a special kind of presence, almost a sacred energy, that seemed to surround me when I was dialoging with different 'symptoms.' And it was this presence that helped me to accept another of Jung's original contentions - that these 'symptoms'/ characters were not problems or dysfunctions that I needed to cure or rid myself of, but instead, they were allies who were present in my life to teach me more about myself and my life. And it was this unfolding sense that helped me let go of any remaining resistance to using this process and also to begin incorporating aspects of the version Andrew Carnegie had used.

From My Dialogues With Merlin To The Writing of This Book

My early dialogues with Merlin were, as you can imagine, often brief and tentative. Indeed, as had been the case in my early experimentation with the Active Imagination Process, I felt reservations and concerns about the legitimacy of my experience. Was it possible to cross the time and space boundary in this way? Was I talking to Merlin, or was I just conjuring up a character in my mind?

Frankly, it was only when I finished one of my longer conversations with Merlin and was reviewing the notes I had recorded that I realized that the information I had received was not only valuable to me in my personal life, but it was also providing me with new and important insights into things that were happening in the world around me.

For example, at that time, Xenophobia as well as Autocracy and its more dangerous cousin, Totalitarianism, were increasing their hold in many countries. And although this same trend was not yet obvious to me here in the United States, there were certainly other signs of the serious challenges present here. Our unresolved challenges with racism and misogyny, for example. There was also our obsessive worship of Profit, Consumption, and Materialism, three concepts that, from the perspectives of many people I admired, were negatively impacting our lives, leading us to endanger other species and to create significant damage to our habitat, which an increasing number of scientists were describing as irreversible. It was also clear that our involvement in nation-building, which had led us into many conflicts, including the Korean War, the Vietnam War, efforts to overthrow governments in other countries, and, if continued, would lead us into new conflicts.

Taken together, these things prompted me to revisit what Jung had called The Totalitarian Virus and what an author by the name of Paul Levy had called Wetiko. In the case of Wetiko, I learned that the Algonquin, Cree and Ojibwa peoples, long before Jung, had also conclude that there was "virus of the mind/disease of the soul' that would, from time to time, cause an individual or a tribe, or in the case of Jung's study of the Nazi scourge, it was an entire nation that failed to acknowledge and work on healing their emotional and psychological wounds. What we today refer to as our shadow. sides

The more I learned about Wetiko and The Totalitarian Virus, the more I understood why so many behaviors seemed irrational and why fear of the other, projection of internal wounds and dysfunctions onto others was becoming so prevalent, and why so many individuals, tribes, and nations were doing or allowing things to be done that were clearly against their own best interests.

The more I looked around at what was happening in the world, and the more conversations I had with Merlin, the more I started to conclude that this "disease of the soul/virus of the mind was not just a psychological theory, but a dangerous reality, and that large swaths of humanity in our time were suffering from this form of insanity.

My Dream and My Next Steps

Time passed. Despite these worsening external conditions, some of the challenges that had led me to seek therapy and experiment with the Active Imagination Process in the first place had improved, and I found that I was making real progress in my writing and in my producing and directing of programs for television. And, to my complete surprise, I discovered that I had both a deep love and previously undiscovered natural skill for sculpting. Another gift that would change my life,

Eventually, I also met and married Sedena, who brought a whole new level of stability, contentment and and joy into my life. And as counterintuitive as this may sound, all of these gifts and genuine gains led me to do what I now realize is something a number of us do. I have heard it referred to as the "Fireman Syndrome." This suggests that when we experience relief from a fire, which can be translated here as a physical, emotional, spiritual, or financial challenge, we turn away from the fireman who reminds us of the previous pain and turmoil, and become complacent and stop doing what we once did to support our healing.

In my case, however, Fate had other plans. A few years later, after Sedena and I

16

moved from Santa Monica, California, to Santa Fe, New Mexico, I woke up one night from a very disturbing dream. Unable to go back to sleep and still feeling unsettled, I wandered around the house until I eventually found myself in my office, scanning titles in the bookcases that lined the walls. I wasn't looking for anything specific. Just something to occupy me. That was when I noticed three unopened boxes in the corner that had been collecting dust since our move. Deciding to investigate, I opened the top box, and to my surprise, found several of the notebooks from my original Active Imagination dialogues with various emotions, and among these were the notebooks containing my conversations with Merlin that I thought I had lost.

Sitting down at my desk, I began flipping through them, and as I did, I found myself intrigued by the content and amazed that I had not been smart enough to continue these conversations. I also began to sense that the dream that had disturbed my sleep with its accompanying sense of urgency had not been a random event but instead had been designed to lead me to rediscover these valuable notebooks.

The more I read, the more I also understood how unique in meaning and scope Merlin's words were. Not only did they express a genuine sense of humility, nobility, and integrity, but they spoke to a much greater level of individual and collective responsibility, he believed every individual should have for the well-being of other people, for the kingdom in which he lives, and for the natural world around him. And this degree of nobility and responsibility was greater and significantly different than anything that I and the majority of my fellow citizens here in the United States were demonstrating in support of our democracy and our way of life at that time.

When I compared this disparity with the events happening in the world around me, especially the threats to democracy that were arising in many countries and, that had begun to rear their ugly head here in our country, I began to acknowledge how much of a decline in ethical and moral values, and personal character, and in the practice of our primary core values, norms and standards had once helped to shape our founding documents. It was also clear that far too many of our so-called leaders no longer seem interested in being public servants but instead have become self-interested political mercenaries, and far too many of us who were citizens had become self-absorbed and seemed to have arrived at a point where we no longer remembered that democracy and the precious rights and privileges that it afforded us was not a spectator sport.

By comparison, the information Merlin had shared with me spoke to a much more stable and constructive way of being, a higher level of personal character, integrity, an honoring of truth, and, of particular importance, a genuine adherence to the values and standards of the Wisdom Traditions.

The more I read, the clearer it also became that my conversations with Merlin were not just designed to introduce me to an earlier historical period or to support me in dealing with my personal life challenges. Instead, they spoke of a level of commitment, purpose, compassion, a deep honoring of life, and a kind of sacred activism that was sadly missing in my life and in our time. And I am now clear that if this trend continues, it will have dire consequences for humanity.

Funny, I don't even remember picking up my pen, but several hours later, when I put it down, I found I had add added notes to a number of the hand-written records of my conversations with Merlin and that taken as whole these conversations amounted to what could rightly be called Merlin's Laws, laws that provided valuable insights and strategies on life, on leadership, and noble governance.

That was when I finally admitted that what had started as an effort to resolve some of my confusions and challenges and to bring greater balance and healing into my life was also providing me with a new focus for my work in the world, and that this work could be advanced by this book.

So, I leave you now to answer for yourself the questions you might have about the validity and importance of the Imaginal/Non-Local Realm vs. what the majority of us call Reality. I also leave you to determine whether the wisdom Merlin communicated to me in our conversations has relevance and value for you, and can also add to your understanding of what is going on in the world today.

It is, of course, also my sincere hope that Merlin's words will prompt you to consider expressing greater creativity in your lives, which is reported to be one of the major cures for Wetiko and the Totalitarian Virus that is currently having its way with so many of us in our time. And lastly, it is my hope Merlin's words will invite you to consider conducting your experiments with The Active Imagination Process and some of the other practices I have mentioned in these pages that can provide you with greater individual and collective wisdom that will better support your life, the lives of those you love as well as those who will come after you, and support you in better protecting the other species and our precious and endangered habitat.

George Cappannelli,
Santa Fe, NM

A Post-Script - Some Additional Information You May Find Helpful

As I began to work in greater depth on my conversations with Merlin and with the laws he had shared with me, I decided to set these conversations not in the contemporary time when I had conducted them, but rather in their original historical period. This decision, in turn, prompted me to add Arthur, the future king, whom I was certain had been the original recipient of this wisdom from Merlin when he was a young man and trying to deal with the challenges that were threatening his world and that he would soon face when he ascended to the throne. And, so it is also my hope that these decisions will support you in enjoying the journey you are about to take and in integrating the advice and guidance offered in Marlin's laws on life, leadership, and noble governance.

For the same reason, I also decided to add a third character who could serve as a kind of narrator for these conversations. And although he began as a purely fictional character, Aderyn quickly emerged as someone integral to this process. He not only began to take a natural role as the scribe who was tasked with recording each session between Merlin and Arthur, but he also became the vehicle that allowed me to establish the time and the physical conditions under which this experience could be described.

And I must admit, as the manuscript evolved, this character took on a life of his own in a way I had not expected. And it is also my hope that he will contribute to your experience in the same way he has to mine.

As my work on the manuscript progressed, I was moved to also add some quotations on life, leadership, and conscious living from other sages and teachers whom I have admired from different historical periods. And I hope you will find that these thoughts, cautions, and insights will complement and reinforce Merlin's content. And, finally, I was moved to create a series of assignments that seemed to emerge naturally from each of the laws, especially as the content expanded and I added questions and comments by Arthur and Aderyn that came up during each lesson, and notes made by Arthur after each session. These mirrored some of the questions and thoughts I had had after my original conversations with Merlin. And lastly, I added a summary of major points within each of the laws to support you in integrating the content.

In closing, I also want you to know that while I have not consulted directly with Merlin in a formal Active Imagination Dialogue about these additions and changes, I'm confident he does not mind my taking these liberties with the wisdom he shared with me. In fact, in that place between the realms where mystery lives and magic often happens, I can almost see a smile forming on his noble face.

Chapter Two - The Law of Firsts

The 12th Century. The Northwest Province of Britain, known as Wales. It is sunrise on a crisp, cold winter's morning.

From high above the Welsh countryside, we see a solitary figure, at first of indeterminate age and size, making its way along a dirt path through a woodland toward a private glen in which an old stone cottage stands, its white plume of smoke rising into the cold, clear air. is nestled

As the figure gets closer, we see that it is a young man wearing a fur pelt coat, hat, and boots; his step crunches the hoarfrost that covers the ground, weighs down some of the branches of some of the trees lining the path, and clings to the scrub ground vegetation as well. As this young man brushes past some of the branches, small clumps of hoarfrost fall on his shoulders and his hat. His breath is also visible in the cold air as he makes his way across the landscape that glistens in the early morning sunlight on this brilliant, cloudless day.

Interior – Merlin's Stone Cottage

Aderyn, Merlin's devoted servant, student, and scribe, is going about the task of putting more wood on the fire, placing three cups of a morning brew of the herbs that Merlin favors. One of the cups he places on the low table beside his master's chair, the second he places on the flat surface beside the chair that has been set up for the young and future king who is currently making his way toward the cottage, and the third he places next to the writing board along with the sheets of parchment, stylus and ink he will use to capture what Merlin has told him will be the first of a series of lessons on what his master has referred to as Laws on Life, Noble Leadership and Conscious Governance that he will begin sharing with young Arthur on this day. There is also a piece of parchment, a stylus, and a small pot of ink that he places on the future king's writing board. Merlin requested that he provide this, in the event the future king would like to record his thoughts and any questions the material may prompt.

As these preparations in the stone cottage unfold, we also see the approaching young and future king, who we can now see is a handsome and vital young man.

Aderyn

For several weeks now, we have been witnessing the early signs of the approaching season, my master refers to as the rebirth of the natural world. However, on this morning, when he and my Liege Lord Arthur will meet for the first of a new series of lessons that Merlin has told me will explore the subjects of life, noble leadership, and conscious governance, the early morning light glistens on what may well be Winter's last display. Hoarfrost coats some of the trees, is visible on patches of ground, and I can now hear it crunch beneath young Arthur's boots as I catch glimpses of him as he makes his way toward the entrance to my master's cottage.

Aderyn Continues as The Young Man Arrives

As my Liege Lord enters my Master's cottage, and takes off his great coat and hat, traces of the hoarfrost that have fallen from the limbs of trees onto his shoulders and head during his walk from the castle fall on the stones of the floor. A little embarrassed, Arthur looks around for a straw broom. Not a usual thing for the future King of the realm to do in the castle, but my Master has introduced him to other rules in his environment. Seeing his discomfort, I reach for the broom I put away earlier and let him know I will attend to it. But his handsome face, red from the briskness of his walk and the cold morning air, breaks into a smile as he takes the broom from me and begins to sweep away traces of the hoarfrost and water. It is another clear example that he takes all aspects of Merlin's mentorship to heart. This action also demonstrates that he is as pleasing in manner and temperament as he is in physical appearance.

As is his custom, when his teacher enters the room, he expresses the honor he always accords Merlin and, in turn, receives a warm, welcoming embrace. This gesture of intimacy is one I have learned that Merlin reserves only for those whom he holds closely in his heart and with whom he works regularly.

I asked him once about this difference in his various forms of greeting that he shares, and he explained that keeping a physical distance from some is not the result of his lack of a gracious heart, nor from his indifference toward them. Instead, he told me that he maintains his distance so the negative and unconscious energies that the vast majority carry in their multiple, non-physical bodies without even being aware of it, will not be transferred to him, and, as a result, not require him to have to do ritual cleansing so he can do the healing that is such an essential part of his work.

While I did not understand the reference to non-physical bodies and negative energies at the time, I have come to understand that Merlin, like others whose work involves the art of healing, must be as clear an instrument as possible.

After I offer the young Arthur a cup of warm water infused with assorted herbs collected by my master, and now, on occasion by me at Merlin's direction, my Master invites the future king to sit in the chair I have placed for him opposite my Master and before the great stone hearth where the warmth of the fire I started hours earlier now gives good comfort.

I also then take my place there as well, slightly distant and yet between the two of them. And when I do this, as is his custom, Merlin invites Arthur and me to close our eyes, take a few slow, deep breaths, and settle more deeply into the moment and our stillness. And it is only when he senses that we have accomplished this task that he begins to speak in his distinct, deep, and sonorous voice that is marked with traces of the grit and gravel of a life lived at great depth and with major consequence.

Merlin speaks softly at first, prompting both Arthur and Aderyn to lean in closer.
And so begins this conversation on The Law of Firsts.

Merlin

Arthur, my boy, there is an ancient proverb that comes from the wisdom of the ancients, which speaks to the spirit of much of the territory we will cover on our journey to explore this subject of life, noble leadership, and conscious governance. And it is this...

> **"It is absurd that a man should rule others,**
> **who cannot rule himself."**

And so I invite you to keep this pronouncement close at hand and let it inform and motivate you as we address a topic today that I believe will prove to be most essential and valuable for you to master, particularly if you are committed to serving those in your care with honor and for their greater good.

I also invite you to pay special heed to the fact that no matter what you may wish to accomplish, be it a small undertaking or one much larger in scope and longer in duration, you would do well to first establish a strong base or foundation on which to build the task. And you can rightly refer to this base as your "first purpose."

Yes, if you are committed to demonstrating nobility and true consciousness, as a man and as a leader, it will serve you well to first identify some of the tools and talents you may need to employ to accomplish your task, and then to be sure to practice these tools and talents so that during the task, you use them with ease and proficiency.

In addition to this step, and before you begin real engagement in any task, it will also serve you to consider a few alternative paths you may take going forward. And I invite you to do this so that if you find one is blocked or it becomes too arduous or indeed, the wrong path, you will have other options.

I also invite you to use the gift of your imagination in this first stage. Visualize at least one and preferably more potential outcomes or destinations. And in doing this visualization, do your best to conjure up the most clear and detailed image of your goal and use all of your senses -sight, sound, smell, touch, and inner feeling. Do this enough so that you will recognize and be comfortable with each possible outcome when you experience them at the time of their physical manifestation.

These preparatory steps, however, should not prevent you from remaining open to discoveries, unexpected intersections, fortuitous alliances, and other difficult obstacles you may encounter. Indeed, each of these things can and will, if you grant them the opportunity, inform your route, as well as fine-tune and even, if necessary, support you in altering your goals, and perhaps, even your reason for doing the task.

Of special note, I encourage you to always take sufficient time in doing each of these things before you attempt the actual physical task or you attempt to enter into relationships with those with whom you wish to manifest things of true and lasting consequence.

These aspects of The Law of Firsts hold for all who wish to undertake any task of any size, but they will be especially valuable for you, as one who will someday lead and serve others in your kingdom.

I also invite you to train in these preliminaries and to work diligently to improve your artful use of imagination on smaller tasks before undertaking tasks that are of greater scope and consequence.

Merlin pauses here and invites Arthur and Aderyn to close their eyes. It is a thing he often does to allow his student and his servant time to reflect on the ground recently covered. And in the silence, he takes the time to study each of their faces and uses his gift of second sight to tune into their thoughts.

Aderyn

It is apparent to me in these moments when Merlin pauses and goes within himself that this silence is designed to allow both young Arthur and me to deepen and refresh our listening. And I can tell from the expression on my Liege Lord's face that he is as grateful for the gift of this opportunity as I am.

It also appears clear from the energy present in the cottage that the information Merlin is sharing is not just coming from him, but rather, it is coming through him. As a result, neither the young and future king nor I is inclined to interrupt him with questions or comments unless he, in one fashion or another, signals his receptivity to such a thing.

And in this moment, I also now better understand why Merlin requested that I give Arthur sheets of parchment and a quill so that he can make note of questions that might arise or other things of special import he can explore with Merlin in later conversations.

This prompts me to reflect on how much care and forethought my Master always displays in his relationship with my Liege Lord.

Arthur, meanwhile, is reflecting on a recent lesson on swordsmanship with his Master of Arms. The thrust and parry of the sword work is suddenly interrupted when the Master of Arms gains an advantage that in an actual battle would have proven dangerous and even fatal to the young man.

Master of Arms

There, right there, note what happened? You did not anticipate that I would move in that way, and your lack of anticipation could have cost you your life. That is why I tell you that you must practice every conceivable response your opponent might employ. And never decide in advance which of these he will choose. As a result, you must practice all of them until your reactions become second nature. In this way, and only in this way, will you be prepared. This is the foundation of your mastery of the sword and of the tactics that will ensure your survival on the field of battle.

Hearing Merlin clear his throat, Arthur opens his eyes to find that Aderyn has also returned his attention to the room.

Merlin smiles and then begins speaking again in that wonderful, sonorous voice.

As a leader, my boy, you will also be wise to avoid the quest for perfection. And in close alliance with this, I recommend you do your best to avoid succumbing to the impatience that haunts the beginning of far too many undertakings, particularly for those who are inexperienced. The first of these, the quest for perfection, is but an illusion that leads most assuredly to failure. For perfection, you see, is not to be found in this physical realm, especially in those aspects created by man.

The second frailty, that of impatience. It is a certain doorway to certain disharmonies that are triggered by too great a focus on personal gain, by the fraudulent belief in easy accomplishment, and by the greed for quick solutions. These beliefs generally arise before the scope of the undertaking is fully understood, and the role of being a servant to the Great Mystery is accepted. As a result, impatience often leads one to wasted efforts and dead ends. Things of genuine consequence and merit always involve significant challenges, unexpected obstacles, a reasonable amount of effort, and sufficient time needed to manifest them. These, you will note, are always essential ingredients in any undertaking process. So always be wary of promises of quick and easy victory, whether they issue from within your mind or are proffered to you by others.

Here, Merlin laughs and, as always, this sound is accompanied by his infectious grin that neither Arthur nor Aderyn can resist.

In the space created, Merlin notes a quizzical look on Arthur's face and nods to the young man, giving him entrance into the conversation.

Arthur

My teacher, your words call up a whole series of occasions when I have expressed both of the frailties you just mentioned. So it is clear that I have much work to do. But is there something I could focus on that might help me better master both of these challenges?

Merlin Smiles

I will answer your question so long as you are aware that, at this moment, it is the second frailty that is, in all probability, motivating your question.

Arthur can only smile at the fact that Merlin, as usual, is always many steps ahead of him.

That is not a criticism, My Son. It is just a caution to notice how seductive and insidious both of these habits can be. So here is my answer, but know as well that it is only one of many possible answers, and you would be wise to uncover additional answers for yourself.

So, one possible way to eliminate these habits is to always remember that it is the journey and not the destination, the process and not the result, that are of greatest and lasting import. For as you will discover, the majority of your life will be spent on various journeys and engagements in search of a multitude of different destinations and goals. It will not, contrary to the wishes and hopes of many, be spent resting on your laurels after you arrive at a destination.

So, I suggest you come to value and truly love all of its twists and turns on the path, even the obstacles and the places along the way, when the next step may be hidden from you or seem impossible to take.

This is the way of life here on this physical plane, and unless you make peace with this reality and learn to enjoy all parts of your journeys, the vast majority of your life will be spent longing after destinations that you may never reach, or that when you think you have reached one, you may end up being disappointed, my boy!

Again, Merlin releases that wry laugh that both his student, and his scribe cannot resist.

Merlin

I also encourage you to put your internal house in order before attempting to order the larger house of your relationship with another, with the greater family called your tribe in this kingdom, and, most certainly, in the greater house of the world. And in doing this, remember that every flaw you may be inclined to believe exists in others or the world around you is most certainly a flaw in your vision or in still unfinished qualities and aspects of your character.

It is why those who know tell us that all beauty and suffering is in the eye of the beholder.

This ordering of one's internal house is, of course, a thing that is far more easily spoken about than accomplished. And doing the essential work on oneself requires time, patience, and great courage. Indeed, my Son, one must learn to always look at oneself and one's motives through the impartial eyes of truth and with sufficient amounts of dispassion and compassion. In this way, and only in this way, will you eventually come to know more about yourself, and through this knowledge come to know others.

In doing these things, I always invite you to remember to first seek and deepen your inner connection to the Great Mystery. And, most especially, hold close your humility and your willingness to understand that there will be many things that you will not and cannot know about how you will fare at various points of an undertaking.

Also have the wit and courage to express good humor about the undertaking and your frailties. This is far more than touting your seeming strengths, for it is *humility* that will keep your path true and your process aligned with the greater good.

Merlin pauses, closes his eyes again, and enters that place within. The silence in the room is pregnant as we become party to Aderyn's thoughts.

Aderyn

As I sit in this silence and gaze from the face of my Master to my Liege Lord's,

I am aware that the good humor expressed by my Master and shared with both Arthur and me is a demonstration of the belief he often holds and often shares with us, that we should never take ourselves too seriously and always steadfastly avoid striving for perfection in the practice of this and the other laws that he will impart. For too much seriousness and too rigid an adherence to any law or rule, as he refers to them, is as foolish as it is impossible.

He generally goes on to say that he cannot stress strongly enough that there is great importance in retaining one's sense of humor in the face of one's limitations, and those of the people we will both serve.

Merlin shifts in his seat, opens his eyes, and takes a long, slow drink from the cup of herbs sitting on the hearth near him, before he begins speaking again.

Merlin

Arthur, The Law of Firsts also advises you to admit what you do not yet understand and cannot yet demonstrate. And, for this reason, do not be afraid to seek the advice of others, at least initially and especially when you are first considering the scope and potential consequences of an undertaking.

I also caution you, however, not to depend solely on the advice of others. Indeed, to be a noble leader, you must invest sufficient effort and commitment in seeking your answers to the questions you ask. Do this through honest inquiry and direct experimentation. Indeed, this is the only way you will be able to evaluate the relevance of the alternatives you uncover, and the only way to evaluate the veracity of the answers and solutions proposed by those who offer you counsel.

And when seeking advice, do your best to do so from individuals of the truest and highest character you can select. For as you have no doubt already begun to experience, there are many whom you will encounter in the world at large who are not accustomed to pursuing paths of original inquiry and unexplored territories. Instead, they are far more comfortable parroting the opinions and the insufficiently explored theories advanced by others.

And many of these others whom they parrot also often remain well within the boundary of the familiar and are motivated more by their need for acceptance and acknowledgment than by their quest for that which is original.

You see, my boy, the discovery of what is original requires discomfort and risk, as well as a willingness to venture into uncharted landscapes – things the majority of those you meet will steadfastly avoid. So be wise and tether the horse of your curiosity and imagination first and finally to the post of inner guidance and personal experience, for this is the truest path to wisdom.

This is not to suggest that theories, opinions, and strategies advanced by others cannot be helpful, particularly when a leader is, as you are, young and without the full maturity of experience. But again, I advise you to avoid relying too exclusively on the theories, opinions, and strategies of others as permanent crutches. Otherwise, you will never develop the strength of your creativity and curiosity, and build strong enough muscles of fascination, innovation, and discernment to support you in accomplishing your mission in ways that advance the greater good.

Merlin pauses, and for a moment looks kindly but with those piercing eyes, first at his young student, and then at Aderyn, before continuing.

Merlin

Above all, remember that to lead is to serve. And that, from the first to the last, we are all in service to something or someone. So, make certain that what you are in service to is of the highest possible order and that you perform this service as a sacred contract with reverence, humility, and gratitude.

33

For that which is highest will never desert you, and your sacred contract will strengthen you even in the face of what may seem like great threats or insurmountable obstacles. While adherence to lesser things will always fall away, that which is truly highest and held as sacred never will.

Those who forget this truth, and other truths contained in the Law of Firsts, too often fall under the spell of the mistaken belief that *they* are superior to and hence hold dominion over others. As a result, in the end, they prove to be fools who barter away their nobility and honor for the price of a modicum of fleeting acceptance and temporal power. As the history of man discloses, these misguided beings generally visit far more harm than good on others, and eventually, on the evolution and well-being of their souls.

Also, know that it is impossible to lead if you cannot follow. Impossible to truly lead if one does not have sufficient practical experience in the undertakings one wishes to lead others in. Indeed, the illusion that a leader learns the art of noble and conscious leadership independently from the arena in which he leads is nonsense. It is one of the reasons so many who call themselves leaders in our time succeed only temporarily, and then primarily in advancing only their own private and limited agendas.

Merlin takes a sip of his herbal brew and looks to Arthur and to Aderyn to see if there are any questions.

This time, it is Aderyn who speaks.

Master, when you selected me, years ago, to come and live with you and become your servant, your student, and scribe, I did not appreciate the enormous privilege you were granting me, nor the enormous distance I would have to travel to leave behind my childish ways and the false beliefs that I was already worthy and capable of serving you.

So, when I hear you say that one cannot lead unless one can follow and that one cannot lead unless they have grounding in the area in which they must lead, I now better appreciate the full importance of your message. And so, I humbly say to you, my Liege Lord, that I have watched many times during your mentorship with my Master that you have demonstrated the meaning of this part of the Law of The Firsts, and I honor you for your courage and your discipline in doing so.

Merlin smiles in acknowledgment of Aderyn's words. And Arthur, a little embarrassed by what Aderyn has said, eventually raises his eyes and nods his thanks.

Merlin

A wise and noble message, Aderyn. One that says as much about the progress you have made as it does about your Liege Lord, whom you honor.

So, another important aspect of this Law of Firsts is about collaboration, mutual support, and acknowledgment of the strengths and sometimes the vulnerabilities of others, things that also say a great deal about the one who acknowledges these things.

Just as the path of self-focus and the quest for personal aggrandizement generally leads, in the end, to the separation from the only true and noble reason for leading, focusing outward and being generous in your acknowledgment will most often lead to greater good and alignment with the Great Mystery.

Another essential tenet of the Law of Firsts is to always trust in the wisdom of the heart. While many believe it is the mind that is the ultimate source of knowledge and authority, the wisdom of the heart is far greater and more stable, for it issues directly from the Great Mystery.

Finally, my boy, remember, above all else, that surrender to the Great Mystery is the shortest and truest path to the full manifestation of any and every goal.

And a path that does not involve this level of surrender will soon pale by comparison. For when a leader surrenders to the Great Mystery, he is greatly supported by it, and all that is required will be revealed and made available to him in right timing and for the greater good.

Merlin stops speaking and fixes his gaze first on Arthur for a long moment.
He then turns his attention to Aderyn and articulates his assignment.

Merlin's Assignment

Betwixt this and our next talk, I invite you to identify one or two undertakings you wish to accomplish and describe how you will go about setting a firm foundation before you begin your undertaking.

I also invite you to reflect on an undertaking you have already accomplished or failed to accomplish and describe how you would have been better served had you first established a firm foundation.

Then he nods, signaling the end of the session. Stands and, without another word, walks from the room.

For several moments, the young men stay in their places, each lost in thought. Clearly, they are both trying to put some of what has just happened into perspective.

Then Aderyn gets up and begins salting the parchment on which he has carefully recorded Merlin's words. Eventually, Arthur stands as well, asks if his two sheets of parchment should also be salted. Aderyn nods and lets the young and future king know where he will store his notes in a niche beside the fireplace. Arthur then reaches for his greatcoat and prepares to depart. Before leaving, he turns to Aderyn and smiles.

Arthur

An amazing session! And this is only the first. I can not wait to see what my teacher has in store for us. And it is also clear that I have a lot to think about this evening, and even more to begin practicing in the days ahead."

Aderyn nods and smiles.

Yes, my Liege Lord, it was, as you say, an amazing session and a very interesting topic that we are exploring.

Arthur nods

Aderyn, I also want you to know that I am grateful for your participation in these lessons as well as your insights.

When Arthur has finished closing his great coat and putting on his fur hat, he smiles warmly at the scribe with whom he has formed a deep friendship over the years and then leaves Merlin's cottage.

As Arthur makes his way along the path through the woods on his way back to the castle, we track his progress. And as we follow him, we become privy to his thoughts and some of the images he reflects on from this first lesson in this new series.

Arthur

Merlin never ceases to amaze me! I have been privileged to experience so much in his presence, and I certainly have to admit that I have, on more than one occasion, been confounded by his many different moods since my father first asked him to serve as my guide and my protector. Most of this time, Merlin has been patient with me, and his intention has most often been to encourage me to seek the best, even if I do not, at first, understand his direction or find his method or tone easy to accept.

On other occasions, of course, he has been intimidating and fierce. Although I must admit that in reviewing those instances, I have always found that they occur most when I am inattentive or resistant, and when he has told me, with little patience in his voice, to set aside my foolishness.

Then, once he recaptures my attention, he pushes me beyond what I think is my limit, and I come to realize I have abilities and strengths I was not aware that I had. I am also aware that he is often surrounded by very powerful energies, particularly when he is engaged in his healing arts or sharing what he calls sacred rites with me and others. But today, the spirit present in and around Merlin captured me differently. And this seemed to be true for Aderyn as well.

Today, I felt that something different was happening as soon as Merlin asked Aderyn and me to close our eyes, breathe deeply, and settle into the stillness. And then, when he began speaking, it seemed as if his words were being spoken from a very deep and distant place. I now realize this will, no doubt, sound strange to anyone other than Aderyn. Yes, it was clear to me today that although Merlin was physically in the room with us, he seemed almost like a kind of hollowed reed through which the words and ideas flowed like a sacred song.

So, while I do not know exactly where this new series of conversations on life, leadership, and noble governance is going or what related assignments Merlin may have for me in the time ahead, I am certain I am entering new ground. I am also sure that the steps he is asking me to take are not those of a boy, but of a man. And I can only pray I will be up to this new challenge and whatever else will be asked of me.

I must also admit that i felt a little awkward today and although I generally avoid the use of parchment and ink when I am in my teacher's company, on this occasion I took his advice to use these tools that Adyern provided me so that I could capture some of my experiences and some of the things he shared this day in this lesson called The Law of Firsts that were clearly of importance.

I have also decided to be as faithful as I can in capturing Merlin's words, for as he has reminded me on many occasions, words spoken have a special significance and should be accorded honor and captured with accuracy. And as I have learned before, his words help me to remember the most important points he shares. They also give me the courage to practice their wisdom more diligently and to complete the assignments Merlin often gives me. Such as the one he gave me today and will, I assume, give me at the end of each lesson.

Up ahead of Arthur, the village comes into view, and above it, the castle in which he lives is visible.

As he makes his way through the village, he greets people along the way, people he will, as Merlin has reminded him so many times, serve, if he wishes to lead with nobility and integrity.

Then, when he arrives at the castle, he is met by his friend and boyhood companion, Lancelot, who exhibits his good spirit and the honor he accords the future king and tells him he has already saddled the horses for their daily ride.

Notes on The Law of Firsts

No matter the task or undertaking, first set a firm foundation in the basics. Always set one's internal house in order before attempting to order the world. Tether the horse of one's curiosity and imagination to one's inner guidance. Remember that to lead is to serve, and it is impossible to lead if one cannot follow, and Surrender to the Great Mystery is the shortest and truest path to the manifestation of any goal.

Chapter Three - The Law of Humility

Do you desire to construct a vast and lofty fabric?
You should think first about the foundations of humility.
The higher your structure is,
the deeper its foundation must be.
-Saint Augustine

Aderyn's Notes

Although the afternoon light is still bright and the air outside my master's cottage carries more of the warmth of Spring, the air inside is still cool and carries traces of the dampness in the stone walls, a reminder of Winter's lingering signature that requires me to continue tending the fire..

This day, there are, as is common in this season, also rumblings in the distance where dark rain clouds have gathered as Merlin and Arthur sit down near the hearth and prepare for their second conversation on this subject that my master has begun to describe as Laws of Life, Noble Leadership, and Conscious Governance.

As my master has instructed me, I have set out another sheet of parchment, as well as a small container of ink and a quill for my Liege Lord to use during the lesson if he wishes to record notes he believes will be helpful to him.

And then, one of the practices that will begin each of their sessions involves my master asking my Arthur to recount one or two of the things he experienced while doing the assignment he was given at the end of the Law of Firsts session.

As is often the case when these two are in each other's company, except, of course, on those occasions when my master believes there is a matter of great consequence or urgency requiring Arthur's immediate attention and a course correction, there is a spirit of ease and good humor present between them as Arthur begins his sharing.

Arthur

In truth, Master, I could not identify any undertaking in the past that I would not have been better had I created a stronger foundation.

Arthur smiles. It is also clear that Merlin is well aware of many of these undertakings, and so he nods in acknowledgment of the truth of Arthur's words and in recognition of Arthur's honesty, a thing he often tells his student is one of his most admirable qualities, and one that will serve him well throughout his life.

Merlin

And what of the second part of the assignment?

Arthur

During our last session, when you advised us to build a strong foundation, I found myself thinking about my last training with the Master of Arms. He had just demonstrated a sword thrust I had not experienced before, one that could have proved fatal in battle, and he advised me that I should practice as many defenses as possible so that I could respond to unanticipated thrusts like that that could harm me. And as I was reliving that training in my mind, I understood that what he was recommending was that I create a stronger foundation with my sword. And in the time between our last session and this one, I have realized that the same is true regarding my horsemanship training, my lessons with quill and ink, my tutoring in our language, in the politics of the court, and in the many things I am being allowed to learn from you. Indeed, the stronger the foundations I can build, the greater the probability that I will become a true land noble leader of my people.

Merlin smiles, then he closes his eyes and calls us to do the same in preparation for the new lesson that is about to begin.

Merlin's Lesson

My Son, on this day, let us talk of humility. As you know, many aspire to positions of leadership or call themselves leaders and believe their role requires them to do battle with life, engineer conquests, and maintain domination over those they lead, as well as over their rights and privileges.

This is an unfortunate thing, for them and, most surely, for those they lead. For, in doing this, they turn life into a contest and, as a result, they seek to control and manipulate not only human resources, but natural ones as well. This, of course, is a fool's errand. For the only thing these efforts demonstrate is that they mistakenly believe aggression to be the path to true power and that by forcing their private agendas on others and by advancing those that favor the few over the many, they will accomplish something meaningful.

This, my Son, as you now know, is a blatant violation of the Law of Firsts by elevating and aggrandizing the self and personal goals over serving the greater good. Unfortunately, this violation is something practiced by a great number who claim to be leaders, and not only in our time but in those recorded on the parchments that are reputed to contain our history. But if one studies these parchments closely and with clear eyes, one can come to see that these illusions, in the end, only accrue that which is detrimental to those they lead, and eventually, to themselves as well.

These so-called leaders also mistakenly believe that pursuing these goals and exercising temporal power in this way demonstrates their strength. Whereas, in truth, they do so to protect themselves against the fear that they are not strong. They also do this to avoid another fear, one that often troubles them the most, and this is their fear of being vulnerable.

You see, My Son, for reasons different in number, but common in source, and most often issuing from some early experience in their lives, they become convinced that vulnerability is a condition to be avoided at all costs rather than one we must all eventually welcome as one of life's greatest teachers. And, it is this attempt to defend against the inevitability of vulnerability that accounts for much of the pain and suffering these individuals experience and eventually try to impose upon others and the world at large.

Those who practice these aberrant forms of leadership also believe it is their responsibility to worship at the Altar of Separation. And one of the greatest sins committed at this altar is based on the belief that they are superior to other men and even to nature, a fraudulent belief that cannot be maintained and that ultimately leads to the imprisonment of the human spirit in the landscape of illusion.

**Merlin pauses, takes a sip from the cup of herbs Aderyn has prepared for him,
Arthur, and then looks at both Arthur and Aderyn to see if either has a question
or comment they care to make.**

Arthur

Master, I am aware, as you speak of vulnerability, that there are many things that I do to defend against it. So much that I have been taught to do, by my father, the King, and his advisors, is designed to be strong.

Merlin

True strength, my Son, has many faces. Among them is the ability to admit what one does not know or has not yet mastered. True strength often comes from flexibility, not rigidity. Consider the reed in a stream, or the sapling in the forest. Those most subtle survive even the harshest of winds. And I invite you to compare the power of kindness, of genuine concern for the well-being of another, and of the value of this Law of Humility we are exploring on this day. Consider the quiet, the softness, the ease of these things versus the harshness and fear used as the instruments to impose one's will upon another.

**Merlin pauses to allow Arthur and Aderyn the opportunity to consider these truths
before continuing to go more deeply into the Law of Humility.**

You see, Arthur, misaligned leaders also mistakenly believe that truth does not exist as an independent force within the Great Mystery, but instead is determined by the number of individuals who can be or have been convinced, manipulated, or coerced into accepting a particular belief.

So be willing to use your eyes to truly see, your ears to not only hear but to listen, and your heart to truly feel. In this way, you will avoid these errant and fraudulent beliefs that, in the end, contribute to the diminishment of all that is unique, miraculous, precious, and original about human existence. Indeed, these errant beliefs can only be maintained when one turns away from, rather than toward, alignment with the Great Mystery.

So if you truly aspire to practice noble and conscious leadership, practice this wisdom found in this Law of Humility and not in the mistaken belief that arrogance and domination will advance your cause. Instead, utilize the Law of Humility as the key to open the door to a more rewarding and successful path forward. Humility will lead you to both invite and demonstrate cooperation, receptivity, and interdependence rather than aggression, resistance, and separation. These latter, as I have said, are but fraudulent imitations of the former.

Yes, humility is a true path forward. And by walking on it with great frequency, you will come to understand that it also grants acceptance, greater tolerance, compassion, respect, and surrender to that which is greater, that which is whole and complete.

It is also true that where arrogance is loud and often raw and gross in its manifestation, humility is more subtle, quiet, non-reactive, observant, and patient. Therefore, humility is much stronger than the fraudulent bluster behind which too many leaders and those they lead come to believe they must hide their fears and mask their ignorance from others. In doing these things, not only do they deceive those they lead, but they also become victims of their own deceit. And in the end, their arrogance and domination prove to be no more successful a strategy than believing that by closing one's eyes one becomes invisible.

By comparison, when you enter more deeply into a state of humility, you will cease to find it necessary to defend your opinions and positions, for the quest of the humble man is truth, originality, and alignment with the natural flow. And not attachment to the illusions of superiority and power.

Merlin, as is his custom, pauses again, closes his eyes, and gives both pace and time
 to both his student and his scribe to consider what they have just heard.

Aderyn

As I study the look of peace on my master's face. I am reminded of another truth he often shares with me. That the knowledge one possesses is, in the end, only as valuable as one's ability to live in alignment with it.

As I consider this, I am also aware that another of the faces my master sometimes wears, especially when I try to offer an excuse for failing to perform one of my duties with care and a commitment to what he calls excellence. When I see that face, there is little doubt in my mind regarding the reason he has achieved such a mastery of life.

Merlin opens his eyes and nods to Aderyn. It is a thing he often does that demonstrates his ability to read the thoughts of others

Merlin

There are other benefits one receives from the Law of Humility as well. As a noble leader or member of the kingdom who practices humility, you will no longer find it necessary to seek after the illusion of control, no longer quest after power for its own sake, and no longer insist that your beliefs are the only right ones. Instead, you will understand that the truth you seek will be found in conditions that promote parity, receptivity, and equality.

So, I encourage you to learn to open rather than close, and not just your mind, but your heart. This practice will allow you access to innocence and the real power of the Great Mystery. Yes, through humility, you will come to surrender your small and temporary goals and instead kneel before the infinite scope and full majesty of the natural flow.

My Son, humility is an invaluable pathway to expansion, fascination, apprehension, and direct experience. Humility will open the door to originality and uniqueness. And it will be a gift that allows you to step beyond the boundaries of the known and the habitual. Humility will allow you to drop your attachment to more limited versions of reality and the need for temporal rewards, which will pale by comparison to all that is expressive, creative, joyful, relaxed, abundant, responsive, and effective. Indeed, in the end, humility supports all in recognizing that all beliefs, accomplishments, titles, and possessions, which far too many seek, are only temporary.

So whenever you discover that these more ennobling experiences are absent from your thoughts, words, and deeds, know that you are out of alignment with the Great Mystery. Then all you need to do to correct this misalignment is to turn away from the illusion of separation, away from the noise and distraction of this earthly plane, and toward the miraculous and far more powerful practice of humility.

In what other ways can humility serve you as well as those you lead to conscientiously seek nobility and higher consciousness? Humility will allow you to understand that whenever the desire arises to elevate yourself over another, this desire will arise primarily from your unexamined fears. So turning in humility toward these fears will help you remember that they are illusions. Humility can also help you remember that the fears that sometimes goad you into trying to exercise control over a person, an event, or a circumstance are bound to fail. For control is an illusion, and its pursuit will only increase your fears. Indeed, in the end, all fears are disguised signs of one's inability to let go and surrender to the limitlessness of the Great Mystery.

So, as one who aspires to noble leadership and those who wish to be loyal and constructive members of the kingdom, I suggest becoming true students of The Law of Humility. In this way, as you gain greater mastery in its practice, you will become a more honest and genuine servant of the greater good with the resources of the Great Mystery at your disposal.

Merlin pauses, takes a moment to look at both his scribe and his student. Then he gives Arthur his assignment, knowing full well that Aderyn will accept it as his as well. Then he nods, stands, and leaves the room.

#####

Merlin's Assignment

Identify five ways you can demonstrate greater humility today in dealing with others and with yourself.

Arthur's Notes Recorded On Parchment Later In The Day

There were times during this lesson today when I found myself thinking of questions to ask Merlin, but that special energy that was again present when he spoke caused me to remain quiet. It did not seem appropriate to interrupt him. So I am making these notes on the parchment to help me remember what I want to talk to him about in the coming days.

His words have caused some confusion in me. Before today, I thought that what I observed in others as humility was weakness. And yet, after listening today, it is clear that Merlin is asking me to consider it a strength. I would be inclined to object were it not for the way he described arrogance. He said arrogance was a loud and crude form of expression. As he said this, examples came into my mind from times when this was an accurate description of my actions. As he said this, I did not want to look at him, for fear he would exercise that ability he possesses to see into my deepest secrets.

But it is most certainly true that, by comparison to arrogance, humility is a quiet, more centered, and pleasing experience. And when I consider moments when I am most subject to doing things that are foolish and harmful to others, things I later regret, I see that these are moments in which I am not centered and am clearly under the influence of what Merlin calls arrogance.

As a result, when I do the assignment Merlin has given me this day, I am certain I will be troubled by the number of times I have failed to practice this second law. For this reason, it seems to me that it will be helpful if I add a second part to his assignment. One that will require me to identify times when my arrogance in dealing with others has caused them and, eventually, me harm. For it not only disclosed my lack of understanding, it also, no doubt, diminished me not only in their eyes, but in my own eyes as well.

Notes on the Law of Humility

Doing battle with life ultimately results in loss not only in stature but in inner experience, particularly for those who wage the battle. The exercise of force and power is a corruption of the spirit and intent of noble leadership. The elevation of self over service to the greater good is a crime. Humility leads to cooperation and receptivity rather than to aggression and resistance. Humility leads to a more expressive, creative, joyful, relaxed, abundant, and successful life.

Chapter Four - The Law of Perspective

"He who has never learned to obey
cannot be a good commander."
-Aristotle

Aderyn's Notes

Although the sun has just begun its descent behind the tallest of the hills that stand at the far and Western end of our valley, my master asks that I set the chairs in place on a small rise that is adjacent to our stone cottage for his next lesson with the young Arthur. From here, one can see some of the lower foothills and the forests that surround our valley.

Except for a few almost transparent clouds that hang near the horizon, the sky is clear and the air warm but not uncomfortable. After my liege lord arrives and my master questions him about a prominent bruise that marks his normally smooth and handsome features and discovers that Arthur acquired it during his morning sword practice, he nods. It is his way of showing that, although he knows this discipline with weapons is required by the King as part of Arthur's training, he often advises Arthur that there are more potent weapons he can master.

Merlin does not stress this, but knowing that he has communicated his point, he then invites us both to enter the place of silence that I so often witness him visit.

And thus he, my liege lord Arthur, and I, who am positioned off to the side with my writing board, parchment, and ink at the ready, sit with eyes closed, and surrender to the sounds of the natural world are rich in their seemingly infinite and subtle variety.

Finally, when each of us begins to more fully settle into the rich presence of the moment, and when each of us, as Merlin has taught us, begins to follow our breath in and out of our bodies, he begins to speak in that special, rhythmic cadence that has marked each of these sessions.

Merlin's Lesson

My Son, when you enter a forest and view it from within its boundaries, it is often impressive but sometimes also a little intimidating, particularly when the size of the individual trees imposes limitations on your ability to gain and maintain a long view of the horizon.

When viewed from a nearby slope, however, the forest appears different to the eye, does it not? The individual trees and the forest itself have, of course, not become smaller in stature, but from this new vantage point and against the backdrop of the hills, the distant plains, and the greater expanse of the sky under which all of these elements reside, the forest and the individual trees seem less imposing. You see, from this new and higher vantage point, you have the benefit of having a greater view of the whole, which can rightly be called perspective.

Therefore, if you wish to lead with nobility, I invite you to remain mindful of conditions and circumstances that obscure or prevent the long view. Be aware that these conditions and circumstances may, at times, cause you to feel overwhelmed, confused, or limited in the alternatives at your disposal.

This limited perspective may also prompt you to act impatiently and before you fully understand the scope of a challenge you face or the unique opportunities a greater perspective will often grant you.

And while the real consequence of premature actions may not be apparent in the near term, over time, one often discovers that such actions have negatively impacted the greater good, not only in your own time but for many others and for years to come. Therefore, be advised that anything that results in the loss of your objectivity and denies you the ability to maintain or regain the right balance and greater perspective should be avoided whenever possible.

Instead, invest patience and seek how you can gain the most expansive and highest perspective. At the same time, complement this greater perspective with more direct experience in the specifics encountered on the ground around you, especially those that impact the lives of those you lead.

As is his custom, Merlin pauses and turns inward. Giving an opportunity to Arthur and Aderyn are to reflect on what he has just said.

In Arthur's case, he finds himself reflecting on a recent ride he took with Guinivere to a favorite hilltop site they often visit. Having tethered their horses, they sit on a stone outcropping that offers a wonderful view of the castle in the distance, the village below it, and beyond this, the lush and wild countryside.

Guinivere

Have you ever wondered what it would be like living out there beyond those hills?

Arthur

As we now are, or as different people?

Guinivere

Different people. If you weren't the future king and I wasn't a Lady in Waiting to your mother, the Queen?

Arthur

There have been more than a few times when I thought about running away and leaving all of this behind. But most of the time, I'm so busy trying to learn to be the best king I can be that I don't even have time for those thoughts.

Guinivere

Well, if you did, who would you be? And who would I be? Would you even include me in your new world?

Arthur

Where do your questions come from?

Guinivere

Your mother says it's all about perspective. She says that the more one considers one's options, the more one knows what one wants.

Merlin opens his eyes and clears his throat.

So where were we? Oh yes. I was about to say that while physical effort is generally necessary and certainly contributes greatly to one's ability to manifest positive results in the physical world, taking sufficient pause and granting yourself a deep and honest surrender to the silence can prove to be another path to gaining greater perspective.

Yes, this surrender to the silence will allow you to accomplish as much and, sometimes, much more than you may at first think possible. Although many who wear this human form are convinced that effort and physical labor are prerequisites for accomplishing various goals, if you practice greater perspective, you will discover that effort and labor are not the only tools to utilize in discovering the essential and most direct paths to follow going forward.

Goals, after all, occur first in the mind as vague images, partial ideas, and fragments of concepts. Therefore, quiet centering, observation, reflection, disciplined focus as well as prayer, a liberal application of imagination, and surrender to the guidance of intuition will contribute greatly to your perspective and provide you with the ability to support yourself and those you serve in accomplishing their essential goals.

Yes, my Son, these tools are powerful and necessary in achieving your desired goals, especially those that may take a long time to manifest. A primary rule that holds sway here on this physical plane is that *energy follows thought, and manifestation follows energy.* Therefore, experiencing energy in both its subtle as well as its more obvious forms and with a long view will always aid your efforts.

This advice is valuable to all who wish to experience lives of greater quality, but it will prove invaluable and essential for you as a leader. Indeed, this advice, practiced best through inner and outer observation, through present-moment awareness, and complemented by the liberal application of imagination, intuition, and a deep confidence in the power made available to each by the Great Mystery, will lead ultimately to right perspective, and right perspective to right action.

On the other hand, be mindful that those who stray from the citadel of grounding in inner conviction and the search for right perspective can become particularly vulnerable to entanglement in the opinions of others, especially opinions and beliefs that are prevalent in their time.

Unfortunately, this practice too often leads one not to the accomplishment of the greater good, but to exaggerations, distortions, false paths, manipulation of truth, and greater entanglement in illusions.

So above all, I invite you to remember that recognition and notoriety, experiences that often pass for greatness in the physical realm, as well as the quest to accumulate more material wealth than is needed and the hunger for temporal power, while also greatly valued by those who wear this human form, things that are often mistakenly viewed as validation of a leader's skills and confirmation of the path he has taken, in the end, are themselves often only illusions. Instead, the real path to achievement for every true and noble leader passes directly through the realm of greater perspective.

#####

Merlin's Assignment

Identify some of the conditions that most often result in the loss of your perspective, including some of the distractions and some of the individuals who seem to contribute most to these. Then identify what you can do to counter these occurrences and thereby gain a better perspective of the situation in any given moment.

Arthur's Notes, Recorded On Parchment Later In The Day

Although I have been following Merlin's suggestion to close my eyes, take a few deep breaths, and settle into the stillness for more than a few years now, I am finding greater value in this suggestion as we go more deeply into these new lessons.

Of course, when I first close my eyes, my mind, as so often happens, my mind suddenly seems full of thoughts. But I am learning the truth of Merlin's guidance that, even though my mind may not stop thinking, I can choose to direct my attention elsewhere. And, when I follow the flow of my breath in and out, I can also direct my attention to parts of my body where there may be some discomfort and do my best to make peace with it or release it.

This was not entirely possible today because of the pain from the bruise on my face, which I received when I let my attention wander during my sword practice earlier in the day. But with some effort, when I focused on the flow in and out of my breath, even this pain seemed to lessen.

So Merlin's suggestions about focus and choice work. This also makes it clear to me that when I come to a new moment or activity still preoccupied by the energy and feelings I've experienced in the previous activity, I miss a great deal of what the new moment offers. Merlin says this is like trying to be in two places at the same time and, as a result, not fully present in either.

As for the topic of this day, the Law of Perspective, I was aware, as he was sharing his wisdom on this subject, that I am often inclined to move quickly into action and, as a result, miss opportunities to do the thing that I have chosen to do or been asked to do with greater excellence and benefit.

So impatience clearly is not my ally. And once again, the lesson of this day not only made this clear but also reminded me that I still have much to learn.

Notes from The Law of Perspective

Always be mindful of circumstances and conditions that obscure the long view. Whenever possible, avoid that which results in the loss of objectivity and balance. Surrender to the silence and inner guidance. They will often offer much more than physical effort alone. Observation, reflection, meditation, prayer, and imagination are essential tools of the noble leader. Always ground oneself in inner conviction and right perspective first. The true path to noble leadership always passes through the realm of greater perspective.

Chapter Five - The Law of Inquiry & Self-Discovery

"As it is, the lover of inquiry must follow his beloved wherever it may lead him."
–Plato

Aderyn's Notes

As is sometimes his custom, my master has been away for several weeks. While I sometimes accompany him on his shorter journeys, there are other occasions when he gathers with other wizards who also explore advanced mystical practices and the magic arts, or when he wishes to journey alone into the wilderness, that I do not. And having served him long enough, I have come to understand, as does my liege lord, Arthur, not to ask him about these solitary travels unless he volunteers information about them.

Sometimes he returns surrounded by a deep quiet, and it is a few days or more before he begins to speak. That has been the case on this occasion, and so I have waited for him to return in spirit as well as in physical form and to tell me to let my liege lord know that it is time for the next session.

It is now early afternoon, and Merlin and young Arthur sit, once again, on the small rise beside the stone cottage, with me in my accustomed place off to the side and between them with my parchment and pen ready.

Sensing that the time is approaching for the conversation to begin and before my master begins his resonant and rhythmic sharing of whatever this day's subject will be, my liege lord recounts an experience he had in losing and then finding a way to regain perspective while completing his last assignment. When he finishes, my master sits silently for a moment and smiles, and nods. It is, as both my liege lord and I know, one of Merlin's deepest forms of praise.

My master then invites us to withdraw to that place of silence within us until the rhythm of our breath and our attention come into harmony with the moment. After a few moments more, my master begins speaking in that melodic cadence that signals the start of the session.

Merlin's Lesson

My Son, before we explore today's law, tell me one of the things that limits your gaining perspective, and something you can do to prevent that from happening.

Arthur

Master, I have again seen that Impatience is one of my biggest distractions. When I am in a hurry, as you have cautioned me that I too often am, I make decisions before I have taken the time to evaluate a number of different options. And in truth, having lived with this inclination for some time, I am not sure what I can do to change this. How to remember to pause, or maybe ask myself additional questions that will prompt me to look further or go deeper.

Merlin

My son, as is my custom, it is not for me to answer this question for you. I can, however, tell you something I do in this regard. First and foremost, when I experience impatience, I admit that it is a choice I am making, and this, more than anything else, opens the door I can walk through to begin to regain power over the moment.

Consequence is another factor, and perhaps one of the most important. When I am willing to view some of the consequences of my actions. Indeed, when I remember that my answers, decisions, and actions will impact not only my experience, but that of you and others who come to me for guidance or healing, I take another step in realigning with the Great Mystery, and I am motivated, as you say, 'to look further and go deeper.

Merlin pauses here. His gaze rests gently on his student, who is looking back at him, but whose focus is inward.

Arthur smiles

Thank you, Merlin. I know that when impatience takes over my attention, it is because I forget that my actions in this time before I assume my duties as king may appear to affect only me, but that is not true. For when I am King, all that I have ever done will be subject to scrutiny and will either advance or retard my ability to lead those who, as you always remind me, it will be my duty to serve.

Merlin nods

Yes, my Son, and this awareness leads us to something that has been said in many ways by many wise ones across the annals of time.. And this message concerns one of the most essential tasks each of us is asked to accomplish during this time when we occupy human form on this physical plane.

This task is to come to know our true, authentic selves by gaining mastery over the vagaries and inconsistencies of our human emotions, like the impatience you speak of. It comes to the fore when we are facing a challenge Fate has placed in our paths, and impatience prevents us from demonstrating the courage to stay with the challenge until it unfolds like a beautiful flower and shows us the best possible choice we can make.

For this reason, I invite you to practice the guidance offered in the Law of Inquiry and Self-Discovery with patience and good discernment. For it is through the practice of the tenets of this law that you and those you will lead can contribute to healing some, and hopefully many, of the wounds that every mortal being carries with them when they enter this physical plane. These, in addition, of course, to the wounds that each of us accumulates from our encounters and experiences with other individuals and events during our journey here.

In this way, you who aspire to be a wise and noble leader can contribute to the elevation of your consciousness as well as to that of those you serve. And in healing your wounds, you, as a leader, will gain clarity and balance for yourself, and this will encourage those you serve to do the same. Instead, as a result of doing this essential personal work, you, as the leader, and those you serve can enter into a deeper alignment with the Great Mystery.

Although this message has been communicated in many different languages by countless numbers of keepers of the ancient wisdom, and, as you will most certainly discover in your travels, this message is found in many and various traditions, rituals, and practices performed, far too many who lead overlook its significance.

So I advise you not to be among those who overlook this message. Instead, pay close attention to the Law of Inquiry and Self-Discovery, for it is vital to your success as an aspiring leader, as well as to those who are already in positions of leadership, and, of course, to all in this and other kingdoms who wish to lead lives of greater meaning and contribution.

So give this law great scrutiny. And remember that no matter how experienced you or those in your kingdom may be in any given subject or practice, no matter how well-schooled you may become or how many other teachers or mentors you may have, and no matter how much success you appear to achieve, the journey of inquiry and self-mastery never ends.

If you and they wish to contribute what is truly unique and valuable to the greater good, you and those you lead are advised to fully explore this law, for eventually if you are true to the call you will pass beyond the protection afforded by other individuals and their teachings as well as beyond all of the practices you normally utilize and you will pass into the unknown. And it is on this portion of the journey that this Law of Inquiry and Self-Discovery will be a most valuable and necessary companion.

Merlin closes his eyes and turns inward, giving pause to his student and his
scribe to reflect on the ground thus far. Arthur also closes his eyes, but Aderyn
shifts his gaze from his master to his liege lord.

Aderyn

This gift of being in service to my Master and in the company of my liege lord never fails to amaze me. Nor does it fail to fill me with gratitude for the grace that has been bestowed upon me by the Great Mystery.

I, who never knew my father and was left behind by my mother, who on occasion prepared food for my master before she passed from this plane, was then taken in by Merlin. Who could have foretold such events, or that I would be sitting here being given access to such wisdom?

Merlin opens his eyes, and as he takes a sip from his cup of herbs, his gaze rests on Aderyn, who brushes a tear from his eyes, and as so often is the

case,

recognizes that this mystical being has been tracking his thoughts. Arthur,
who has opened his eyes, sees this exchange between his teacher and the
scribe.

Merlin

So if we are to fulfill our destiny and serve the greater good, we must all
ultimately step beyond the currency of ideas, beliefs, and habits that are
familiar and prevalent in our time, and in this new territory we will be
challenged to ask and answer the primary questions that each of will hopefully
have addressed before, but because they are both essential and timeless, we
will be best served by exploring them again.

Who am I? Where did the beliefs I currently hold come from, and how do I
validate their authenticity? What is the purpose of my life and of life itself
in this new time? What constitutes right action in this new time? How do
I learn to truly live with an open and neutral heart even in the face of these
new challenges that Fate is presenting? And, in your case, as a leader, how
do I best perform my function as a servant of those I lead?

Addressing these and other primary questions, again and again in the
different phases and cycles of our lives, lies at the very heart of the reason
we come into this life and wear this human form. Yes, these questions are
essential stepping stones on which each of us must walk to reach new levels
of consciousness. And for this, the Law of Self-Inquiry and Self-Discovery
will not only be a guide but a prerequisite, especially for those who truly seek
alignment with the Great Mystery in which there is no such thing as status
and no final destination, only the natural flow, which is constantly evolving.

Merlin pauses and looks to Aderyn.

Aderyn, you have been quiet this morning. Tell us, what do you make of this

Law of Inquiry and Self-Discovery?

Aderyn, surprised by Merlin's Question, but well-trained by his master, takes a moment before responding.

It seems to me that in this time, even here in our kingdom, where we are blessed with both a wise king and my liege lord who will one day, I am certain, nobly serve our people, that the reaction of many is to look outward for answers to the challenges we face, and as a result recognize the importance of this Law of Inquiry and Self-Discovery. And this makes your sharing of this ancient law of great importance.

Merlin looks first to Arthur, who is nodding in acknowledgment of the truth, Aderyn has just spoken. He then turns to his scribe and, with his eyes, communicates his appreciation of this young man's gift of maturity and his willingness to speak of such things in the presence of this young man, who will someday be his king.

Merlin

Another important consideration regarding The Law of Inquiry and Self-Discovery is to remember that these questions asked and the answers gained should not be adhered to with rigidity, even within the cycle in which you and those you lead address them.

Instead, I advise you to treat each as a valued ally, utilize the information you have received from them with both curiosity and humility, but also be attentive to the twists and turns in the road and the moments in the cycle you are in when early signs of possible change may begin to present themselves. In this way, you and those you serve will know that it is time to again pay close attention to the Law of Self-Inquiry and Self-Discovery, for each turn and twist on the road of life requires new answers and sometimes significantly different strategies.

Indeed, as is clear from even a cursory observation of the natural world, a stream forded or path walked upon today is not the same stream you forded or the path that you walked upon yesterday, nor will it be the same one you will ford or walk upon tomorrow.

Yes, just as the clouds that cover the sun and bring moisture at this moment are not the same as those that did so on past days or will on future days, you are advised, as part of your inquiry and self-discovery, to stay alert and observant in each present moment. In this way, you will know when it is time to ask these and other questions again. And even if it appears that you are getting similar answers to those you received in the past, take the time to appreciate that they may have a different context and meaning, and perhaps will require a slightly different interpretation in the way you implement them.

Yes, each answer you and those you serve receive has a unique and different value relative to the moment or period when you and they asked your inner oracles for guidance. And each message you receive, like that stream or cloud, is distinct and offers a different challenge or potential outcome. This understanding of the constant ebb and flow of life, which truly is the essence of natural law, will allow you to learn, not just to deal with the when and how of change, but to appreciate and celebrate it.

Indeed, the greater the integrity of your inquiry, the greater the probability that you will discover greater flexibility and become more comfortable with ambiguity, which is one of the true gifts of life and an essential condition you would be wise to honor in your study of the natural flow.

These are just a few of the benefits you will gain through the practice of the Law of Inquiry and Self-discovery. This law will also help you become accustomed to changing directions and revising strategies based on the constantly changing information and signs that disclose themselves to you.

And, you and those you lead will be encouraged in this way to explore and experiment with a range of different methods and processes, which will allow you to become even more fluent in the language of change.

So, I advise you to stay in touch with the ever-changing flow of the natural universe and come to understand that this flow is a valuable doorway to the Great Mystery. Do this, and you will be greatly aided in your efforts to serve the greater good. Indeed, the natural world is a teacher of immense value, for it models the always-evolving, never-static requirements of the path on which you, as a leader, and those you serve will walk toward lives of greater nobility and consciousness.

Here, Merlin pauses to allow his scribe and his student the opportunity to digest some of the essential points made.

Arthur, meanwhile, finds himself remembering a time several months ago when he and his father, King Pendragon, were returning from a trip to the North to visit one of the king's most important allies. The meeting had gone well, and so the King was in very good spirits, so he and his entourage had stopped beside a bubbling stream to water their horses and rest for a while. During the stop, his father asked Arthur to walk with him.

King Pendragon

So my son, what did you make of our meeting with the Duke?

Arthur

It appeared to be successful?

The King

You say "appeared." Did you not believe that to be the case?

Arthur

I did not find the Duke forthcoming. Nor do I believe he will keep his agreement regarding his defense of our Northern Border.

The king studies Arthur for a while before responding.

That is very perceptive of you, Arthur. Clearly, your time of study and tutelage with Merlin is serving you and the kingdom well. Yes, you are growing up, My Son. And while I am not certain you are yet ready to send me off to my dotage, I do believe that time is approaching.

You have become a good student of the natural law, and contrary to the beliefs held by many in this time, it is that law, far more than the law invented by men, that you can rely upon. Well done, Son! Well done!

Merlin opens his eyes and makes a point of creating a little noise when he reaches out for his cup of herbs. The noise calls Arthur back to the present moment.

Merlin

Did you have a good visit with the King?

Arthur smiles, not surprised by the fact that Merlin has, as he so often does, tracked his inner thoughts.

Yes, Merlin. I did.

Merlin

Good, because the next part of our talk today is about avoiding being deceived by those who pretend that returning to the past or seeking to maintain the status quo are valid options. As you discovered on your trip with your Father to visit the Duke, true adherence to the Law of Inquiry and Self-Discovery will reveal that the past is a text to be studied and its lessons applied in the present. But it is not a condition one should seek to take up permanent residence within. As we have talked about and you have experienced, the status quo is not a condition found in the natural world. Hence, the quest for it, which is also called stasis, leads to stagnation, which, in the end, is another of the illusions advanced by those who search for another of the great illusions called 'safety.'

Therefore, attempting to lead on any current day based primarily on the conditions you experienced yesterday or attempting to lead by clinging to the illusion of what you and those you lead have done in the past will only result in you and those you lead falling victim to the futile practices of those who believe it is possible to enter the future by walking backward.

You see, My Son, stasis, constancy, the illusion of stability that is unchanging, which is what you took note of in the Duke's proposal, as well as the search for safety that he is constantly advancing, are the artificial creations of those of us who wear this human form and who keep vainly looking for surety and simplistic answers to address a mystery that is beyond their comprehension.

Indeed, this effort represents frail and futile attempts to protect what is at best a false understanding of the Great Mystery, and as a result, leads to the conjuring up of fantasies and pretenses that far too many in our time seek in the hope that others will believe that they control themselves, others, and the natural flow. itself

Many among us, particularly those who lead without nobility, act out this and other fantasies and advance these false beliefs about control and safety by treating the many contradictions and irregularities of Fate and the natural world as exceptions to the rule. Worse yet, they do their best to deny the existence of change and ambiguity by establishing laws and policies that are both unnatural and rigid, as if that which is rigid could ever survive in the natural world.

This absurdity will become more apparent to you as you look with eyes willing to see, hear with ears willing to listen, and feel with an open heart. In this way, you and those you lead will avoid the illusions that those who are blinded by self-serving agendas and narrow beliefs suffer. You will also avoid the inclination to propagate misinformation in the hope that it will provide you with the illusion of the legitimacy of these kinds of self-serving agendas and narrow beliefs.

So practice this Law of Inquiry and Self-Discovery, and you will avoid the all too common inclination to lead by exercising force and power and the dark arts of manipulation to retain a hold over those you lead or to hold on to a position that, in the end, can only lead you to inflict pain and suffering on yourself and those you serve.

On occasions, and these certainly arise from time to time on the path that even the noble leader travels, when you find yourself tempted to succumb to the lure of these illusions and their false promises of easy and quick results, you can regain your perspective and balance by returning your attention to the silence and the observation of natural law. Natural Law always speaks of flow and alternation in rhythm in the constantly shifting tapestry and magic that is life.

So, my son, let change be your path, inquiry be your compass, and let curiosity and fascination guide your decisions and your commitment. Let the desire to learn and to know yourself and the world in which you live be your constant goal at each step during this blink of the cosmic eye that is your physical existence on this earthly plane. In this way, your time at the helm will be marked by wonder and exploration, by discovery and unfolding, and the fruits of your service to those you lead will rightly and proudly be celebrated as your legacy – a legacy that will eventually be amplified and expanded many times.

#####

Merlin's Assignment

What are some of the primary questions that can assist you to better know yourself, your role in this kingdom, and on this physical plane itself?

Arthur's Notes Recorded on His Parchment, Later in the Day

Even with that special energy present during Merlin's lesson on this day, I had trouble, at first, focusing my attention. It was only when my teacher's words prompted me to realize that my lack of attention was not caused by other thoughts as much as by the fact that I was avoiding dealing with the subject he was exploring. As soon as I realized this, I found it a little easier to pay attention.

It then became clear that Merlin was speaking a truth that I had avoided in many ways and on many occasions. Particularly when I am unwilling to look at my thoughts and actions and to acknowledge a truth about myself that I find hard to accept. And yet, it became clear as I listened today that it will be difficult, if not impossible, for me to know another and their motives if I am unwilling to accept my own, no matter how distasteful it may be. And it follows that to avoid what the Law of Inquiry and Self-Discovery will disclose will make it impossible for me to better understand the ebb and flow of life and more of the Great Mystery.

Yes, it was also clear to me that the world, as Merlin has always told me, is in some ways far more complicated and in others not as complicated as some would have me believe. Merlin always laughs when he tells me that by making things complex, some people believe they are making themselves appear more intelligent and important.

I wonder if these people know this to be true or if they, like me on many occasions, miss both the truth about life's simplicity and their need to make themselves appear more intelligent by making things complex. For this is true for me as well, and much more often than I admit.

Notes on the Law of Inquiry and Self-Discovery

To know oneself and gain mastery over the inconsistencies of human emotion is the true path of leadership. To meet one's destiny, one must step beyond the boundary of current ideas and concepts that mark the boundary of the known. Self-awareness and self-discovery are the faithful allies of the noble leader. The ever-changing flow of the natural order is the doorway to the Great Mystery. The laws of the Great Mystery are the true laws. The desire to learn and know should accompany the leader in all stages of his journey.

Chapter Six - The Law of Initiation

"You know, after any truly initiating experience,
that you are part of a much bigger whole. Life is
not about you henceforward, but you are about life."
–Richard Rohr

Aderyn's Notes

The rain and fog that have been our constant companions for more than a week now, a normal occurrence here in late Summer, have finally passed. As a result, the morning is alive with color and the fragrant scent of the earth that is well-nourished and made even more fertile by the moisture.

My master often uses these occasions to lead us in search of the plants that are necessary for the various healing potions, salves, and mixtures he prepares for those who come to him for healing from within this realm and from distant kingdoms.

And on this day, the treasures we harvested were plentiful, so he is in a particularly good temper when young Arthur arrives for his session.

When my liege lord arrives, however, it is clear that he is troubled by something, and so, I think it best to allow him to share whatever is burdening him in private. As I am leaving the cottage, I hear that the trouble involves Guinevere, the young woman of noble birth for whom Arthur has developed a genuine fondness.

I am therefore surprised when my master calls out to me to return only a few moments later. And when I enter the cottage, I find the young Arthur and my master laughing heartily. Knowing my master's rich experience with those of the fairer sex, I do not doubt he has provided my liege lord with precisely the antidote he needs to resolve his confusion.

They are, in fact, still laughing as my master directs us to our places, closes his eyes, drops down inside himself to that place of sacred focus which reminds us to do the same, and then begins the next lesson.

Merlin's Lesson

Arthur, we have talked briefly about your last assignment. I wonder if you have come to any more realizations about some of the questions you can ask to deepen your practice of the Law of Inquiry and Self-Discovery?

Arthur

Yes, Merlin, I have discovered that there are questions. Not just about what my role can be, but how I can better demonstrate my willingness to serve those who will swear their allegiance to me as they have to my father, when it is my time to take my seat on the throne.

And I must admit that when those words sound in my mind, they give me great pause. For there are many days when I am sure I am not ready for that task.

Merlin

Arthur, if you did not have these doubts, I would know for certain that you are not, and might never be, ready. to assume your role as king. But the level of inquiry and self-discovery demonstrated by your doubt gives me, and I know your father, confidence that on the day you are called, you will assume the throne with a level of humility and integrity that will serve you and those you lead well in the years ahead.

For in many ways. My Son, you have been preparing to do so since your birth. First by observation of all that transpired around you, then through the guidance of those who have served you during your early years at the castle, and then during the years you have studied with others who have given you practical guidance in the many skills you must have as a prince and future king, and then in our years together in which you have undergone numerous and more formal rites of passage and initiation.. And if you now come to look upon your ascendancy to the throne as another initiation, then you will be well served.

Unfortunately, in these awkward times, there are far too many who aspire to or hold positions of leadership who are not open to guidance, have not passed through such rites and initiations, and are therefore much the poorer for it. As, of course, are those they lead.

This is a telling fact, for as we had spoken of previously, whether these rites of passage and initiation are masculine or feminine in nature, they are essential to the maturation of the individual and to the development of genuine character, two prerequisites for noble and conscious leaders.

And it is most unfortunate for many other kingdoms and the natural world itself that many who rise to positions of leadership in our time are born into lives mistakenly called privileged, and, therefore, they gain access to positions of power not through merit gained through rigorous initiatory challenges. Instead, they inherit positions they neither fully understand nor have earned. And therefore they and those they lead suffer.

Others gain access to leadership as a result of cunning and malfeasance. Others use their ability to influence the minds and hearts of others through the practice of the dark arts of sophistry and false promises about their abilities. Sometimes individuals gain leadership positions as a result of their ability to manipulate the levers of what is called commerce, which in its basic form is barter and trade that, when well practiced, allows all to acquire the goods and services through equity and good trade. When misused, however, it results in unnatural personal gain and advancement of the few over the many.

Still others rise to positions of leadership primarily as a result of their misuse and abuse of the wealth they have not earned, but have inherited and therefore do not truly understand or appreciate it.

And finally, some do not fall into any of these categories, but as a result of a serious unbalance of temper and lack of alignment with the Great Mystery, resort to the use of force and aggression to gain dominance over others.

In the end, however, leaders who gain their position by any of these means that do not include their passage through genuine rites of initiation end up demonstrating a deficiency of skills and the absence of essential qualities of character and vision that are prerequisites for those who seek to contribute to the greater good.

As a result, these individuals lack a true understanding of what is required of them to be true servants of those they lead. Yes, leaders who have not participated in rites of passage and initiation, and their number is increasing all the time, also do not have sufficient opportunity to confront their inner wounds and flaws, and conversely, to experience and expand their strengths. Hence, they suffer from one of the great afflictions of this or any time - the failure to have genuine empathy and compassion for others and for themselves.

These so-called leaders also suffer, of course, from a lack of true perspective and, as a result, are inclined to revert to the use of subterfuge, deception, manipulation, fear, and force as the primary strategies that allow them to gain and then exercise control over those they lead rather than granting them greater empowerment that allows all in the kingdom to grow and to prosper.

Merlin pauses here, and as he has demonstrated during the sharing of each of the preceding laws, he closes his eyes and turns inward. As he looks up from his parchment and studies both Merlin and his liege lord, we are privy to Aderyn's thoughts.

As I look around this cottage and reflect on the years I have spent serving my master, I realize that while I have not experienced some of the initiations that my liege lord has, in many ways, every day has involved some form of initiation into the art of service, and when that has not been the case, I have been initiated into some level of the healing arts, the collection and use of the herbs as well as the art of seeing and so much more.

And when I think about the awkward child that I was when Merlin first chose to undertake my care and my training, I am certain that the things he has already said about initiation and the many other things he may speak about in his articulation of the Law of Initiation will be both enlightening and true. For in so many ways, my entire life has been in his service, and so long as my master allows me, I will gladly remain so, and welcome being involved in one level or another of initiation,

Merlin opens his eyes and returns from that inner place of quiet to which he so often journeys. For a moment or two, he remains silent. Then he nods and smiles to Aderyn in acknowledgment of his scribe's thoughts about initiation, Then he leans forward and reaches for his cup of herbal brew, which alerts both Arthur and Aderyn that he is ready to begin speaking again,

Merlin

My Son, in ancient times, when sages and wise ones ruled, this form of unearned leadership was more the exception than the rule. In that time, young boys and girls were, from the moment of their births, exposed to the wisdom and mentorship of these elders. Indeed, it was the custom, even the moment of their birth, as was the case in your life, that was witnessed by elders like me, whose task it was to identify the unique gifts each child carried with them onto this physical plane for the well-being of the kingdom.

That was true for every child, no matter their station or reach. And, this sacred role performed by the elders was considered of essential value to the stability and future well-being of all.

At its foundation, this role also involved supporting the child to identify his or her unique gifts, and then helping them to acquire the requisite skills and qualities of character needed to share these gifts with others for the greater good. Hence, it was considered both a critical and essential role for the elder and the child.

In the case of children, like you, who were born into lives of station, their initiations began early and first involved the provision of nurturing, encouragement, and establishing trust. Then, with this foundation in place, the role of the elder could evolve into one like that which you and I are now experiencing.

In this stage, my role is, of course, to share instruction, offer counsel and guidance, and through special initiations that expand your skills and help you amplify and expand positive traits of character, as well as your understanding of the primary workings of the Great Mystery.

Eventually, a relationship, like ours, includes the design and oversight of still more significant rites of passage and initiation that each young person and especially aspiring leaders require before being recognized and acknowledged as an adult member of the kingdom. In this way, adulthood is earned and not simply acquired as the result of physical growth and chronological aging.

As Merlin continues to describe the gifts the initiate acquires, Arthur finds himself experiencing images from some of his more rigorous initiations.

Merlin

Rites of passage and initiation are, as you now know, designed to test the student's mastery of life's essential lessons and increase his or her ability to deal with the illusions of fear that arise, either frequently or periodically, for all who wear this human form. Initiations and rites of passage also allow the student to confront the unknown and challenge their illusions about separation and permanence. And, these confrontations with essential aspects of the Great Mystery are, as you have discovered, vital to deepening the student's direct experience of their inner resources - ingenuity, imagination, discipline, compassion, patience, humility, and, courage - which in all cases are essential allies on the path of those who wish to or are called to become responsible members of the tribe. They are also prerequisites for all who wish to truly serve and enter more deeply into the Great Mystery.

Rites of passage and initiation also expose the student to some of their deepest fears and doubts that, if left unexamined and unmastered, will prove to be impediments to both their maturation and to the development of that which is called true ethical and moral character.

Rites of passage provide the initiate with the opportunity to develop greater self-awareness and to understand how to deal with many of the limitations that arise when human emotions and negative thoughts are triggered by encounters with the challenges Fate presents along the path of life. Rites of passage and initiation, therefore, allow the student to learn how to exercise greater discernment and self-discipline. Skills, qualities, characteristics, and experiences that are essential to all who aspire to live a life of true meaning and purpose, and especially to those who wish to lead.

Rites of passage and initiation also allow the student to better understand the source from which their illusions of doubt and separation arise. And, these rites of passage also allow them to discover within themselves new resources, strengths, and skills that they do not know they possess until they are tested. Finally, these rites require the student to learn how to read the signs of the Natural Flow, and confront and master significant obstacles – sometimes even those that relate directly to their ability to survive. As a result, the student who undergoes rites of passage and initiation is better equipped to explore the Great Mystery and to ascend to levels of leadership that benefit the whole.

Arthur brings his attention back to the cottage and to Merlin's continuing description of the importance of initiation and sacred rites of passage.

My son, from these rites of passage and initiation, also comes to a deeper understanding of the infinite reservoir of inner guidance available to everyone and its paramount importance, especially to those who wish to lead lives of genuine value. Indeed, not only does this reservoir grant the necessary strength to hold steady on the path of wisdom, but it also gives the initiate a greater capacity to avoid being led astray by false and transient emotions or the more superficial desires and limiting agendas that preoccupy many who do not fully understand the preciousness and brevity of this opportunity to wear the human form and use this time to elevate one's consciousness.

Initiation also helps the student to honor his elders and to protect and preserve the wisdom tradition that is always available to those who have the humility to ask and the courage to surrender.

Merlin pauses here to see if there are any questions or comments his

scribe or student
wishes to make. This time, it is Aderyn who speaks.

Aderyn

My teacher, the deeper you go into your sharing on this Law of Initiation, the clearer it becomes that for these and other reasons you name, it is important that all of humanity should mourn the absence of these rites of passage and initiation and do what can be done to reinstate their practice.

I am, of course, aware that my liege lord will have it in his power to do some or all of this, but how do I and others of normal status in the kingdom contribute?

Merlin

First, by being aware of the importance of continuing these sacred rites and practices. Next by demonstrating in every encounter with others, and most epecially with the young, your skills and contributions, and doing so slowly enough to invite their interest, pointing out the benefits in a way that allows them to recognize the merits of developing similar skills and then, when they ask providing them with specific support and instruction to allow them to develop their version of these skills and competencies,

Another way I suggest you both contribute to encouraging a return to the practice of rites of initiation is to remind all in your immediate circle that education does not end when we are young, but instead that all of life is a school in we who wear this human form are given opportunities in each moment to learn unlearned lessons from the past and new lessons for the future.

And in this way, Aderyn, you and Arthur can contribute to the renewal and expansion of these sacred rites and initiations.

Arthur leans forward

Master, I have also heard you comment on what you have suggested is the corruption of education. Would you say more about how this relates to stimulating the practice of sacred rites and initiations?

Merlin

Education originally was intended to develop in the young the ability to call forward wisdom from within themselves, but instead it has become a means by which the young are domesticated, encouraged, and rewarded for mimicking the habitual and limited practices and beliefs of the day.

Yes, this so-called education bypasses the identification and development of each child's true and unique gifts and instead encourages a form of false fealty to that which is known and familiar, and to that which, in turn, perpetuates the illusion of safety and the 'status quo.'

Yes, education has become a form of instruction that encourages greater addiction to the illusions and false promises of advancement and progress. It also encourages the pursuit of goals that are primarily external, temporary, and exclusively temporal. These, unfortunately, have become, for far too many, the primary means by which they measure their worth. And included in this measurement of worth is the motivation to accumulate material wealth, the elevation of the self over others, and the illusion of success through the acquisition of power, all of which, unfortunately, involve the sacrifice by the individual of true originality, uniqueness, and the expansion of higher consciousness. This, of course, is true at this time for the majority of those who lead as well as for those they lead.

So I say to you both, soon you will be given the opportunity to serve others, and if you wish to do so with genuine nobility of purpose and excellence, identify steps in the evolution of leadership you may have missed, seek to develop new and more conscious skills as diligently as possible and, everywhere and on all occasions, treat each encounter, event, and experience as a rite of passage and initiation. In short, use each encounter, event, and experience as an opportunity to learn, to test your will and ability to move past the illusions and fears that dominate so many in this time.

Seek ways to immerse yourself in the world in which those you serve live. Observe, understand, and experience what it is that calls up their frailties and fears, that serve as the objects of their dreams, that constitute the challenges and obstacles they face, and that also, beneath and between all of these things, expose the similarity of their needs, and the true longings that issue from the depths of their hearts. This experience and investigation will be a gift of inestimable value that you can contribute to this time in which you live.

And, lastly, and of special import, look for guidance, not solely from those who are familiar and similar to yourself, and certainly not from those untested and still confined within the habitual practices and beliefs of this day, but from those who carry gravitas within themselves and have been tested and who, as a result, better understand the purpose and meaning of life.

In short, acknowledge the gift of privilege and the opportunities present in each moment. Treat each moment as a deeper initiation in the School of Life, and, in this way, seek ways to atune more deeply to the natural law and to the true and timeless wisdom of the Great Mystery.

#####

Merlin's Assignment

Name several events that occur daily in your life that you can use as rites of initiation, and speak to how you can best identify what lessons can be learned in each.

Arthur's Notes Recorded on His Parchment, Later in the Day

If I had not experienced some of the initiations and rites Merlin has required of me, I know I would still be as much a boy as some of my peers who have not experienced these rites and will one day inherit their realms, which will be the poorer for it.

For this reason, I do not look forward to the time when I will sit in counsel with them. I know it will not be easy for us to come tan o accord on issues that are of great consequence. For as Merlin has said, those who do not pass through rites of initiation grow in physical stature, but in spirit and intellect, they remain immature.

This also makes clear to me why some who come to court seeking favor or resolution before my father, the King, often appear to be like large children who come wearing the disguise of adults.

And, as I reflect on this matter, I am aware that this is sometimes the case with me as well, particularly when I do not get my way. It is then that I find myself behaving like a small boy again. So, one of the questions I now see that I must answer is how, when it is my time to serve, can I find a way to eliminate this tendency within myself so that I can encourage those who have grown physically, but not in other ways, to do this as well?

Notes on The Law of Initiation

Identify the ancient ways and rites of passage and initiation. Where none are immediately present, seek out those who still practice this necessary art of turning inward for guidance. Look to the School of Life to provide ample clues as to where the true risks are that will test you. Pay attention to the natural flow in each moment to guide you. Always seek that which elevates, deepens, enriches, and expands one's consciousness, for these are the true rites of passage. Always remember that wisdom is the gold to be discovered on the path that is life.

Chapter Seven - The Law of Fascination

"Boredom and fascination are opposite sides of the same condition
Both depend on being outside rather than inside a situation
And fortunately, the first eventually leads to the other."
  − Arthur Schopenhauer

Aderyn's Notes

My master is in especially good humor this early afternoon as he awaits the arrival of young Arthur. When I asked him earlier whether he would like me to set up the chairs in the cottage or out on the rise, he surprised me. Certainly not an uncommon occurrence in my dealings with this sage.

Instead of suggesting any of the previous arrangements, he asked me to make it possible for him, my liege lord and I to meet at the top of the ancient watch tower where in prior times, members of the King's brigade had stood watch to warn people in the castle that stands atop the highest hill in the area, as well as those in the village and the surrounding valley of any approaching danger.

When I tell him I will and ask if he wants me to notify my liege lord about this change, he tells me that it will not be necessary. Instead, he suggests that after Arthur arrives, the three of us will take advantage of the beauty of the early Fall afternoon to walk to the tower.

He smiles when he tells me that he is certain the expansive view of the colorful tapestry made by the turning leaves will be a perfect backdrop for the afternoon's conversation.

So now, as we settle in here atop the watch tower, my master calls us first into the silence and alignment with the Great Mystery before he drops even more deeply within to begin speaking from that sacred space.

Merlin's Lesson

My Son, as we look out this day upon this land, more resplendent than the most colorful and artfully tapestry ever woven by the hand of man, I invite you to allow your sense of fascination to surface and consider that in this human realm, we who wear this human form do things for many reasons, and the majority, if not all of these reasons, issue from what we have been taught to value by those who came before us.

It is, however, unfortunate for the majority of us who are alive today that many of the reasons and values that guide our lives today are no longer based on natural law and are not, therefore, fully aligned with the Great Mystery. As a result, they do not introduce us to the kind of true beauty and wonder that awakens our hearts like this vista that spreads out before us, which is a gift from the Great Mystery and is the basis of the law we will explore today.

Instead, too many of us in our time have learned to focus on and value external symbols of achievement that have been created by man, are disconnected from Source, and therefore are far more transient and temporary.

We learn to quest after what we call wealth and possessions in many forms and to look for forms of tribute and accolades that are arbitrary, constantly shifting, and, unfortunately, in the end, often prove to be of far less or no value at all. We also learn to chase after many other illusions - power, control, safety, security, surety, and domination of others - believing these things and other temporary and arbitrary accolades will somehow help us to fill a longing that, unfortunately, will never be satisfied by any of these things.

To compound matters, this pursuit of wealth, material possessions, and external signs of temporal achievement is advanced by leaders who, far too often, are chasing the same illusions and dangle these signs like shiny beads in front of us. Temporary signs that do not encourage our practice of the highest virtues and qualities that those of us who wear these human forms are capable of, but instead only perpetuate our sense of inner lack, perpetuate our hunger, and fail to heal the inner wounds we want so desperately to heal..

Instead, it is only by aligning with the Great Mystery, which neither demands nor requires external signs and symbols from us to validate our intrinsic worth, that we and the leaders charged with guiding us will be able to stop chasing these illusions and start discovering the true wealth and treasures we already possess.

This is a very troubling truth, particularly in this time, when more and more of these external signs and symbols of temporal achievement are endorsed, reinforced, and encouraged by the members of our family, by others in our kingdom, and, most especially, by leaders who are themselves held prisoner by these very same misunderstandings and illusions. Hence it is easy to understand why they, in turn, use the promise of these symbols as the primary means of motivating our fealty, and when these promised rewards fail to accomplish this – as they all eventually must – it is both regrettable and sad that these leaders most often revert to the use of fear and eventually to physical punishment, which they administer under the authority of laws generally of their design.

All of these things, in turn, further domesticate the majority of us, usurp-ing our energies and talents and dulling our life force, robbing us of our sovereignty. and directing our attention away from the pursuit of our true dreams and aspirations that are imprinted in the design of the life we are born to live. They also obscure our innate sense of empowerment, our passion for higher consciousness, and, unfortunately, prevent us from seeing that we, and our leaders, have lost our way.

So if you truly wish to be a noble and conscious leader first become aware of your frailties and those places where you are constrained by limited beliefs, habituated practices, deficits of character, unhealed wounds, unmastered emotions and unfulfilled needs hat would have you and others pursue these external signs of temporal achievement in an attempt to fill that which cannot be filled in this way.

Merlin pauses here, takes a sip of his refreshing herbal brew, and directs his
attention to Arthur.

Arthur, in our last session, we spoke of the Laws of Initiation, and I asked you and Aderyn to name other forms of initiation you could both practice and encourage. How does this subject of fascination fit into that scenario?

Arthur

My teacher, you have often spoken of the role curiosity plays in luring us beyond the known and the limited beliefs that obscure our sight and give us entrance into uncharted territory. Today, you speak of our quest for temporary objects and forms of recognition that cannot, in the end, fulfill our true needs. So it seems to me that fascination is a close companion to curiosity, which, as you have so often said, is the cure for boredom, and that thankfully, there is no cure for curiosity. So I can only then assume that the same is true for fascination and that the practice of fascination is another form of initiation.

**Merlin laughs, and as always, the sound is infectious and invites both Arthur and
Aderyn to join him.**

Merlin

My Son, I must admit that you have become very adept at finding innovative ways to answer my questions. So I say, Bravo! But I also remind you to be sure to use your true intelligence, and always measure your response against the voice of wisdom that is within you, so this valuable and evolving skill does not turn into a form of sophistry.

Do you understand?

**Arthur nods, aware that he has just received another
gift of great value from his teacher.**

Merlin

Good, so let your skill direct you and those you lead to follow the wisdom of your heart. In this way, you will practice the Law of Fascination and allow it to draw you and all who you lead toward that which is unique and original, to that which is another of the portals to the Great Mystery.

By comparison, a focus on a destination, on result, reward, accumulation of possessions, and other forms of human preoccupation, or the doing of something out of fear of punishment or concern about the possible loss of acknowledgement, will always limit your ability and that of those you lead to uncover their unique gifts.

External focus on these things will also restrict your ability to take risks, to seek out less-traveled and unexplored paths, and thereby limit your chance of discovering what is beyond the borders of the known. Even ordinary reasoning makes clear that if one is focused on a result, then it must be something that is already known.

So as a future leader, one of the true gifts you can share with those you serve is to invite, inspire, and encourage them to follow the call of curiosity, imagination, and intuition, and fascination, all things of a similar nature and lead toward originality and authenticity and to travel into the territory of unknown, and feel the excitement of risk and the wonder of discovery.

These are all signs that you and those you lead will be practicing the Law of Fascination. These are also ways you will not only connect deeply to the true rhythms and pulsing of life, but you and they will be advancing the greater good.

Yes, it is through understanding and practicing the Law of Fascination that you can experience the joy of play and celebrate the wonder and adventure of discovery. It is the Law of Fascination that will allow you and those you lead to experience genuine gratitude, celebrate, surrender, honor humility, and remember that true guidance is always available from the Great Mystery. for those willing to seek it

These, My Son, like the wonders that are spread out here on this day with such beauty before us, are signs of paths I encourage you to follow and to support others in following as well. For it is on these paths that one can gain access to and take up true residence in the realm of the mysterious, the magical, and the enlightened,

And while these paths may sometimes lead, at least at first, to things that may not yet be well understood and, as a result to what may initially call up derision and criticism from those who have never taken a true risk or traveled out beyond the boundary of the habitual and the familiar, I assure you that if you remain true to The Law of Fascination and hold a vision of the greater good in your heart; if you encourage those you lead to stay true to their inner call as well, eventually you and each of the individuals you serve will arrive at their next destination enriched, expanded, and in greater alignment with the natural flow.

And if individual rewards accrue along the way to you and others who are being true to the Laws of Fascination – as they often do – you will be wise to remind yourself and those you lead that these rewards can be received with gratitude, but they should not become the sole reason for the next great adventure and discovery.

This is important advice, my Son. Using any other means to motivate yourself or others will only be temporary. Indeed, those you motivate with the promise of temporary glistening lures and illusions or through threats, punishment, and loss will grow accustomed to expecting these rewards in greater quantity or will require larger amounts of fear and punishment to motivate them.

By comparison, if you invite yourself and those you serve to explore The Law of Fascination, you will support the breaking of the addictions to many of the illusions that imprison humanity and the quest for the Fool's Gold of temporary rewards that result in the loss of individuality, originality, greater consciousness, and true alignment with The Great Mystery.

For a few moments now, I invite you to close your eyes and call to mind an experience that approximates, in its way, some of the wonder, beauty, and mystery you have viewed from this tower this morning.

Arthur's Vision

A summer morning just after the sun has begun to make its way above the horizon. A light predawn shower has covered the grasses and leaves with a thin coat of moisture that the morning light ignites into countless numbers of jewel-like reflections that sparkle in the still, cool dawn air.

Merlin walks ahead, his steps measured and soundless on the moss and needles that coat the ground. Arthur follows him, and Aderyn is close behind. All three have empty sacks tucked into their belts, into which each hopes to put the herbs for nourishment, as well as those that will be mixed by Merlin for some of his healing rituals. Merlin has an additional sack across his shoulder for these special herbs.

From time to time, Merlin stops and, without making a sound, points to the presence of a small fox with a remarkably full tail and very large eyes that are watching. A little further along, he points to a glen filled with clusters of vibrant colors captured in the rays of morning sunshine filtering through the trees. A little later, he pauses as they approach a small stream that is meandering its way along the forest floor. Here, a small herd of deer, a mother and two young fawns, stop their grazing, ready if need be to flee. After deciding that the three visitors pose no threat, they return to the grazing as Merlin leads them on.

Having covered a distance of a few miles from the cottage, Merlin leads his student and his scribe into a portion of the forest that neither has even visited. And it is here that they begin to see significant amounts of rich, green moss covering the fallen logs and the exposed tree roots, and, in some cases, the lower trunks of the older trees as well.

Although the sunlight does not penetrate as freely to the ground in this section of the forest, the light that filters through the trees high up has a magical quality to it, as does the song of the birds, who are surprisingly plentiful and diverse.

Merlin pauses and gestures for Arthur and Aderyn to come closer. And in a voice that is barely a whisper, he speaks.

Merlin

This is a very sacred place. It is the home of the Elementals, including both the little people and the fairies that I have, from time to time, told you about. Together, they are responsible for the health and well-being of the forest. So we must honor their home, and when we pull up any of the herbs we will find here, we must offer and blessing and disturb the ground as little as possible.

And when we go around that next turn, marked by that large fallen tree, we will not speak in our tongue, and I will instead, by gesture, indicate which herbs to pick. These you will put in the sacks you have tucked into your belts. Many of these will be the herbs we drink for our nourishment, and that I use for potions I make for those who come to me for support.

I may also leave from time to time to go in search of the other herbs that I require for other rites and rituals I perform. If I do, I ask you to remain silent and to limit the speed of your movements and your steps, for you do not want to injure any of the Elementals who reside here.

I do not know if any of the guardians of this sacred place will show themselves to you. But if you are open and will use the form of seeing that I have shared with you both, you may be gifted with their appearance.

What then follows is a time unlike any that Arthur and Aderyn have experienced before. Although both have spent countless hours roaming the woodlands around the castle and the village, they have never before visited a place like this, and are both stunned and humbled by its beauty and magic.

And when their arrival and their practice of the form of seeing that Merlin has taught each of them is honored by glimpses of several faeries, who favor them with smiles and gestures of welcome, both Arthur and Aderyn

As Arthur reflects on this experience, he is deeply grateful to Merlin for making it possible for him and Aderyn to step across time and into an alternate dimension that parallels our own.

**Merlin clears his throat and calls both Arthur and Aderyn back to the present
moment and then concludes the session with his next assignment.**

\#\#\#\#\#

Merlin's Assignment

Identify occasions in which your focus on reward, the approval of others, or domination over others has failed to bring you inner peace and ease. Then identify a few instances in which fascination has helped you to stay true to the harmony of your nature and in connection with the Great Mystery.

Arthur's Notes Recorded on His Parchment, Later in the Day

After this day's lesson, I find myself troubled by what Merlin said. He told me that most of the things people do, they do for some kind of reward. At first, I did not think his words applied to me, but the more I reflect on this, the more I realize that most of what I have done in my life, I have also done for rewards. Even if the reward has not been immediate but was placed there, like a charm at the end of a pole and a line, I have, like a fish in the stream, too often followed it for a great distance with it as my only focus.

So now I am beginning to see that what Merlin said is true for me as well, and I realize I must explore the remedies he offered. I must learn to do the things I do for the love and joy of doing them and for the greater good of others and of myself, whether others approve and even if there is no visible reward.

I know, of course, that this new understanding is much more easily met in my mind than in my daily actions. And yet it is clear that it is necessary to begin somewhere. For if I am to encourage those who will someday view me as their leader, to do things for the love of doing them, I must master this challenge in my own life first. And I can already see that this is no easy task, especially when I consider how often I and others I know betray each other by holding out those poles with lines and shiny charms attached.

And I must think more deeply about this and talk more with Merlin about it. It seems that encouraging myself and others to do things for the love and joy of doing them rather than for a reward will require a great change in the structure of my life. And at this moment, I do not know how or if I can accomplish this. But if what Merlin has said about the transience and ineffectiveness of pursuing false signs and symbols is true, then I must surely do what I can to make this change before I am given the opportunity to lead.

Notes on The Law of Fascination

The Great Mystery neither demands nor requires symbols or signs of human achievement. Leaders who seek external signs and symbols are often driven by an internal lack. Noble leaders recognize that their frailties and imperfections are gifts leading to higher levels of consciousness. The enlightened leader seeks to educate and empower those he leads. Fascination, play, adventure, wonder, and the willingness to surrender to inner guidance are keys. Rewards are only the byproducts and not the reason the noble leader acts.

Chapter Eight - The Law of Knowing & Not Knowing

"The only true source of wisdom
is in knowing you know nothing."
–Socrates

Aderyn's Notes

The winds are blowing from the North today, and my master reminded me earlier that they are not only the harbingers of Winter but also prompts regarding the preparations those of us in this kingdom must make to be ready for this harshest of our seasons. The time ahead, he also reminded me, will be marked by less freedom and ease of movement in the world around us, and when the availability of game is reduced, the plants needed for my master's potions and brews will become harder to find. Indeed, a time when our people as a whole are often challenged.

These winds have been blowing steadily for several days now, so I replenish the wood for fire in the main hearth and set the chairs in place close to it, as I will now do this day's lesson between Merlin and young Arthur and all that will follow.

And now, as Merlin begins to speak. I note that his voice is deep and full of emotion, like the winds that are buffeting the cottage and causing the limbs on the trees close by to move in sweeping arcs across the outside walls.

My liege lord, it seems, is also in a serious mood. This becomes apparent when Merlin asks him first about his experience with his assignment on The Law of Fascination. Arthur responds by saying that he has discovered that far too many of the things he has done in his life have been motivated more by the desire for reward and recognition than by true immersion in the action or task itself, and, clearly, not out of fascination for what could be learned.

My master nods his noble head and then, reaching out, pats Arthur's hand. Although he does not accompany his action with words, this gesture seems to be enough to confirm to Arthur and me the value of this understanding that Arthur has reached. And I can see by Arthur's reaction that he is touched by Merlin's praise and reinforced in his commitment to pursue this path of leading with nobility.

Merlin's Lesson

My Son, it is indeed not easy to separate oneself from the beliefs of the human herd, for there are many apparent advantages to being a part of a herd. And man, although those of us who call ourselves such do not believe this to be the case, is most certainly included within this category of herd animals. The comfort of numbers, the benefits and joys of companionship, and the information and knowledge we accumulate through social interaction with others of our type also constitute herd characteristics.

There are also the benefits of having access to a variety of skills and the myriad abilities and talents that are distributed among the members of the herd to which we belong. Lastly, there is the strength of numbers that allows herds to accomplish things that solitary animals alone cannot.

There are, however, also several limitations inherent in the lives of all herd animals, as any of us who take the time to observe their behavior with honesty and patience can attest. And if you choose to remain committed to noble and wise governance, you will recognize that close and careful observations of these limitations are a worthy pursuit.

These limitations appear to arise from the behaviors many in the human herd come to believe must be practiced to ensure their continued acceptance and belonging within the herd. Unfortunately, these behaviors and habits – among which are the delegation of sovereignty, the repression or modification of seeming differences, and the sacrifice of many forms of originality and uniqueness – too often become the price members of the herd believe they must pay, often without being fully aware of the real cost and the long-term consequences of these prices.

This is a truth demonstrated and, unfortunately, perpetuated by many leaders of herds as well as by those whom they lead. It should also be noted that in this human variation of the herd, there are many beliefs present that are not found in other herds in the animal domain, where the power of reasoning, as defined by humans, is neither present nor falsely celebrated.

Merlin pauses and turns inward to allow both his student and his scribe the opportunity to reflect on what he has said. In silence, Arthur finds that his head is suddenly filled with images depicting examples of the herd **behavior Merlin has suggested from time in the marketplace among the people he will someday lead.**

Men are posturing and competing for attention and recognition from other men. And behaviors that are even more common in the presence of women. Women at the community wells and at the river's edge, where they gather in smaller groups to wash their clothes and gossip, showing favor to some and excluding others.

Other images from his life in the castle, couriers going to great lengths to gain the attention and favor of the king or others at court whose rankings are greater than their own. The relationship and what can certainly be called the pecking order, long established and rarely questioned, but often resented by the younger Ladies in Waiting interacting with those who have held their positions for many years, and the same is true for other servant groups.

He sees images of children playing, competing, and often fighting with each other and mimicking the actions of adults. He also sees images of himself and his peers competing with one another as much for the attention of other young men as they do for the favor of young women.

Indeed, the more these images flash across the screen of his mind, the more certain Arthur becomes that Merlin's definition of the herd-like quality of human beings is not only accurate, but impossible to refute.

Merlin reads the consternation on Arthur's face.

It is a mixed blessing, isn't it, Arthur? The trick is to witness, but not to judge what you see. To observe and let your discoveries inform and guide you, but not to cause you to separate yourself from others. You see, there is much to be gained if you honor, appreciate, and capitalize on the advantages of herd behaviors - including some of the gifts I identified earlier: the collective skills, the community support, the ability to do together what cannot be done alone, the safety in numbers, the comfort of human interaction, etc. It is the other side of the coin - the limited beliefs, the group conformity, the rigidity of thought that one is advised to move beyond.

Although Arthur is accustomed to Merlin being able to track his thoughts, he is still surprised by how transparent his inner feelings are to his teacher, including conclusions that, in some instances, he has not yet even arrived at, but when Merlin describes them, he knows them to be true.

Merlin

Among these limited beliefs are many that, over time, have produced self-perpetuating, restrictive fears and illusions. And the most debilitating of these are those that encourage and even appear to require us to pursue safety, security, and control as our primary goals, which have value within the bounds of reason, but too often become obsessions that greatly retard one's experience of life. In addition, there is the belief found among members of the human herd that one must become something other than what one was born to be, and that one must keep pursuing and becoming this other something if one wants to continue being a part of the herd.

Taken together, these and other limiting beliefs and illusions greatly compound the challenges members of the human herd face. And I call them challenges because they contradict Natural Law, which speaks to a profound and fundamental truth. Through birth, one enters into a life experience in which there is no guarantee of safety, security, or control. And on the question of belonging, even the most cursory observation of Natural Law demonstrates that one already belongs, simply by virtue of one's birth. Therefore, one requires neither the permission of permission nor some arbitrary level of accomplishment to earn the right to be what one was born to be.

If you think back on the ground we covered in our session on The Law of Initiation, you will remember that in ancient times, it was the role of the elder to attend the birth of new members of the tribe and to help them identify the unique gifts each child brings with them when they enter life. So the current fraudulent belief that one should pursue safety, security, and control, and that one needs to become someone other than who we are at birth and pursue paths that are different from the gifts and dreams our hearts call us to pursue, is truly a self-inflicted crime committed by far too many members of the human herd. And this crime results in great discomfort, dissatisfaction, suffering, and ultimately, what is perhaps the greatest sin of all, the failure to inherit our gifts and develop the skills and talents to share our dreams with others.

These fraudulent beliefs and the associated practices that issue from them also prompt the majority of herd members to stay within carefully prescribed boundaries and habituated practices, practices that are not only rigid and uncomfortable but contradict the laws of the Great Mystery, which instead advance flexibility, spontaneity, self-empowerment, and joy.

Merlin pauses again, and seeing that Aderyn has put down his quill and is leaning forward in his chair, nods, encouraging him to enter the conversation.

Aderyn

Master, as I listen to these things you are saying about the limitations we, as members of the human herd encounter, and as I reflect on the fact that from our earliest moments, the majority of us learn by observing and copying the behavior of parents and older siblings and being told by these individuals what to do and are punished when we do not, it seems a difficult and often impossible task to break free from what you call limiting beliefs and behaviors of the herd.

In my case, I was blessed and fortunate that you agreed to take me in so early in my life and that you encouraged me to learn by making my own choices, and very often my own mistakes. But this is not true for the majority of our people. So, are there additional suggestions you can offer us regarding how they can benefit from the parts of being a member of the herd you mentioned, but avoid the limiting beliefs?

Merlin smiles.

A good and fair question, Aderyn. One way this can begin to happen is when our young and future king, and eventually you, at a different level, begin to educate those around you regarding the strengths and frailties of the herd mentality, and the difference between believing and knowing. You can do this first by demonstrating the joy and benefits of following the dreams that lie in your heart and not succumbing to limited beliefs that would have you blindly following the beliefs of others rather than your own knowing gained from direct experience.

I grant you that in this age, when there is such rigidity of thought and often a demand for unquestioned obedience, this is no small task. However, if you remember that what we are discussing is a path that can lead you and the people of this time into a new age, an age of greater freedom, personal empowerment and a way of living that is more egalitarian, you will have greater patience with the effort and become way showers for other who also wish to explore their original gifts and share them with others.

I advise you, keep your own counsel, do not flaunt a willfulness in the face of those who demand absolute fealty, but instead let the joy of your accomplishments and the value of your skills speak for themselves.

A second way you can become a way-shower for us is to avoid one of the most dangerous frailties of herd mentality. And that is our addiction to seeking and needing the approval of others for what we do and for what we appear to know.

This tendency is, of course, also all too present and, sometimes, of even greater detriment, when it is present in the leader of the herd. Not only does it demonstrate to those he leads that they should do the same, but it becomes a serious deterrent to the leader's ability to recognize the many ways a leader gives away his authority and his agency by depending too exclusively on the approval of his subjects. This is not to say that a leader should not gauge the well-being of those he leads as a means of determining the effectiveness of his leadership. But there is a significant difference between gauging the well-being of one's subjects and falling victim to the flattery and manipulation by those who are seeking to influence a leader for their benefit..

So beware of your for approval and acceptance, for it can make you the prisoner of shifting loyalties of those you serve, rather than emerging naturally as a result of your wise and good action.

When this search for approval applies to the members of the human herd, this search often results in too-easy a delegation of their sovereignty to the other members of the tribe and to leaders who too often abuse it. In addition, this delegation often involves the denial of or the significant diminishment of the unique gifts that each member of the herd possesses and is born to develop and to contribute to the greater good of the greatest number.

Another limiting behavior both leaders and members of the human herd too often practice is their mistaken belief that by adopting the limited beliefs of the herd, they are being good members of the herd. This is simply not true. The true contribution each member of the herd can make is to seek direct experience of the natural law and contribute their discoveries to the herd as a whole.

And here I encourage you to make a major and true distinction between what often passes as knowing – generally the accumulation of information – rather than 'true knowing' - which can only be gained from direct experience, and from the willingness to pursue the path of self-inquiry and discovery. Knowing also accrues to each of us when we spend sufficient time going inward into the silence, and when we make it our goal to search for harmony and alignment with the Great Mystery. There are essential steps that lead to wisdom.

So like other human herd behaviors, that I have called limiting, the tendency on the part of both the leader and members of the herd to worship believing above knowing, to confuse the accumulation of information with the acquisition of knowledge and wisdom, results in the defense of the familiar at the expense and encouragement of the new, the original and, most particularly, the mysterious and the sacred.

So always remember, at their best, beliefs are only temporary conditions or resting places on the path to greater knowing and, ultimately, to genuine wisdom. It is also true that untested beliefs are the most troublesome and potentially dangerous to one's well-being, especially when they are tightly held. And, tightly held beliefs become rigid, and as we have discussed in our previous sessions, rigid beliefs do not endure in the natural world, where flexibility and suppleness are the ultimate strengths.

So, if you wish to practice noble and conscious leadership, my Son, I encourage you to avoid governing based on the amount of approval you receive. For as is clear to those with eyes that can see as well as to look and ears that can listen as well as hear, approval is a constantly changing, often unstable, and elusive metric and not nearly as valuable as respect and loyalty. These expressions come from being a faithful servant of the Great Mystery and practicing authenticity and integrity of being.

So, my Son, always seek direct experience of the natural laws and allow them to deepen and mature into wisdom within you. Also, be willing to move past the false positions of certainty that often accompany beliefs and instead acknowledge what you do not know. For nothing undercuts the position of a leader more than the awareness on the part of those he leads that he is unwilling to admit what he does not know. And, nothing elevates a leader more, in the eyes of those he leads, than the courage to admit what he does not know and the willingness to ask and to learn more.

This is why there are so few good leaders in the world and even fewer leaders who can be called wise. Indeed, it is this failure to understand and practice this Law of Knowing and Not Knowing that causes many who find themselves in positions of leadership to resort to subterfuge, aggressive manipulation, intentional deceit, and when these things fail, to introduce fear and force to maintain what could and should be maintained effortlessly and easily through the exercise of curiosity, humility and the wisdom.

These latter qualities will come naturally and always to those who remember that leadership is not about power but service, not about privilege but purpose and vision, not about self-aggrandizement and the advancement of private agendas, but in pursuit of the greater good.

So hold close the tenants of this Law of Knowing and Not Knowing and let it support you in remembering awareness that noble leadership and conscious governance are not based on information that Noble and conscious leadership is based on discernment, accumulated practical experience, compassion, understanding, a deep and genuine commitment to empower others, the pursuit of fascination, and your willingness to surrender to the Great Mystery.

Demonstrating these and other uplifting qualities and practices, you will most surely manifest your dreams and support and encourage others to listen to the call of their dreams, celebrate their originality, and contribute their best to the highest good.

#####

Merlin's Assignment

Take some time between this and the next lesson to discover how much easier it is for you to identify with those who know rather than those who believe.

Then do your best to discover where the beliefs you hold come from. Whether they still apply to the life you are now living or primarily to the life you were living at the time you were introduced to the beliefs. And also do your best to determine how you can separate what you know from what you believe.

Arthur's Notes Recorded on His Parchment, Later in the Day

It is strange to think of myself as a herd animal, but on this day, as I listened to my teacher's words, I knew he was speaking the truth. Whether the herd is small like a family or large like a tribe or indeed like the kingdom itself, many of the things I and those I observe do are similar to what I see the hens, goats, and cattle in the village do. And this applies even to the wild fowl that visit the ponds in the season of the harvest. So, as much as I like to think I am different, more independent, and somehow superior, Merlin is right in saying that we who wear this human form surrender many valuable things to gain the approval of others and to avoid being looked upon as outcasts. And the thing that troubles me greatly about this is that this surrender seems to have become such an accepted and natural thing. So I wonder, if it is even possible to enjoy the company of others without delegating this thing Merlin calls my sovereignty, to them?

And what about my relationship with my father, the King? How can I retain dominion over myself and still pledge fealty to him? And when the day comes, when I become King, how do I support and encourage others to retain sovereignty over themselves when they pledge fealty to me?

I am beginning to see why Merlin says this is no small or simple matter and why so many who lead succumb to the temptation to avoid empowering the people they serve, and instead treat them as animals in a herd.

Notes on The Law of Knowing and Non-Knowing

Never depend on the approval and acceptance of others as a way of validating the self. Learn to differentiate and demonstrate the difference between believing and knowing. Forgo the temptation to pretend that information alone has value. Seek direct experience and true knowledge as the direct path to wisdom. Celebrate uniqueness and originality, and encourage others to live out their lives in this way. Noble and conscious leaders must never be afraid of admitting what they do not know.

Chapter Nine - The Law of Connection & Relationship

"We cannot live only for ourselves. A thousand fibers connect us with our fellow men, and among those fibers, as sympathetic threads, our actions run as causes, and they come back to us as effects."
-Herman Melville

Aderyn's Notes

Although the morning is particularly cold, my master has decided that he, my liege lord Arthur, and I should take a walk in the woodland surrounding the cottage before beginning the next conversation about leadership.

I start to explain that this will make it almost impossible for me to be accurate in capturing his words, but he only smiles and encourages me to have more faith in the power of my ears to listen and in the ability of my mind to remember.

I am about to object, but his smile becomes a laugh. It issues as that wonderfully deep and infectious sound that I have discovered is impossible to resist. And then he does what he often does: he invites me into a deeper understanding of his purpose. The walk he tells me is not intended as a time to share something that must be recorded on parchment, but instead is designed to allow our hearts to commune with the natural world. It is also designed to interrupt my liege lord's expectation and alter a pattern he has become accustomed to. For when we are given the unexpected to deal with, he tells me, when an anticipated pattern is altered, we tend to become more attentive and receptive.

He also tells me that I should not be surprised to discover that some of what we might say to each other during the walk might be echoed when we return, for while men like to think that their words are distinct and precious, in the end, truth is a relatively simple thing and is generally found in multiple forms that are shared with us by The Great Mystery over and over again.

As Merlin speaks, his eyes hold that special sparkle that always precedes moments when he breaks into his irresistible laughter.

As a result, when my Liege Lord arrives and is about to take off his great coat, I notice the surprise on his face when Merlin suggests we begin our time together with a walk. And as we set off, I notice that, as my Master predicted, young Arthur continues to pay even closer attention to Merlin. His curiosity is stimulated, and his interest is focused.

And Merlin, of course, appears not to notice any of these things. Instead, he makes what appears to be a series of non-related comments, pointing out this or that cluster of the flora in the landscape. He also takes time to point out some of the small animals and birds we encounter and talks about the beauty of the light that is illuminating everything it touches on this brisk morning.

And now that we have returned from our walk, taken off our great coats, and sought out the warmth of the fire, my master once again calls us into the silence before he begins today's lesson.

Merlin's Lesson

My Son, the cold of this day could easily have caused us to become more rigid in our movements, prompting us to try to withdraw from what we perceive as discomfort. But viewed from a different perspective, the cold allowed us to wake up and, instead of restricting our movements, prompted us to increase them in order to stimulate our energies and produce more heat in our bodies. For it is movement and action, engagement and openness to whatever is happening around us as well as within us that ultimately contribute most to genuine warmth.

This is true as well when it comes to our topic today, a topic that is closely allied with the Law of Knowing and Not Knowing. And incidentally, do you have anything you would like to report on how you differentiate between those who know and those who rely primarily on belief?

Arthur

Yes, I am always amazed by how much of the ground of my life is based on beliefs. This always becomes clear when I take even a little time to listen closely to things that I or others say, at court, in the marketplace, in the village, or when I am with my close friends. And that doesn't even begin to allow me time to discover where these beliefs come from.

Merlin smile

Yes, I understand. So let us reserve some time later to go more deeply into your experience, but for the moment, can you give me one way you have found that you can separate something you believe from something you know?

Arthur

Feelings, I think, are my best clue. When someone is speaking from a direct experience or what you have called knowing, there is a different sound in their voice. And I don't know if this makes sense, but the sound seems to come from deeper inside them. I guess I would say that it is clear they have had a direct experience of what they are sharing.

Merlin smiles and nods.

Good, very good work, Arthur. And we will go more deeply at another time, for this is a most important subject and a key step on the road to living an authentic and original life.

For now, however, so let's turn to today's topic - The Law of Connection and Relationship. And, if you want to understand the full implications of this law, I encourage you to consider that just as the Law of Firsts advises us to always seek to establish a firm foundation or base before embarking on a task or undertaking, this new law advises us to always first seek to establish a good and caring relationship with oneself before seeking to relate to or to lead others and. most certainly, to learn to relate to others before seeking relationship with the whole tribe or kingdom.

A good and caring relationship with oneself is also achieved through move-ment, action, engagement, and openness. It is achieved by being willing to keep an open mind and to shift and change perspectives, as we did during our earlier walk. In short, our walk, which was a departure from our usual beginning, captured our attention and also helped to sharpen it.

So now we can explore this Law or Connection and Relationship with an uncluttered mind. We can also better understand its relationship to a number of the previous laws we have discussed – The Law of Firsts, The Law of Humility, The Law of Perspective, The Law of Inquiry and Self-Discovery, The Law of Initiation, The Law of Fascination, and The Law of Knowing and Not Knowing.

Yes, My Son, a good and caring relationship with oneself requires the development and practice of sufficient amounts of patience, observance, curiosity, honesty, humility, passion, fascination, creativity, self-acceptance, and, above all, courage.

A quality relationship with oneself also takes time, the willingness to take risks, the development of an appropriate amount of discernment, and the desire to gain and demonstrate emotional maturity. And these skills, of course, result from our willingness to observe ourselves in each present moment without judgment. They also allow us to learn from the experience of what we consider our breakthroughs and victories, and what is most valuable. A quality relationship with oneself also comes from observing those actions and experiences that many of us mistakenly refer to as our mistakes and our failures. And to do these things with clear observation and without judgment. For judgment always calls up emotion, and emotion often colors our discernment and clarity.

In this way, we come to know that discernment and clarity allow us to understand that our seeming victories, as well as our seeming mistakes and failures, are vital and complementary elements in our education on life. We also come to understand that the ground of the self is precious. It is sacred ground on which the natural laws can be understood and, ultimately, if one is willing and committed enough, mastered. It is also the ground on which the personal wounds that accompany the majority of us who occupy this human form when we gain birth in this physical plain, as well as the other wounds we accumulate along the path and that exhibit themselves as negative emotional reactions, fears, doubts, illusions and limiting beliefs and habituated behaviors, which once identified and observed, can eventually be integrated, accepted, healed and released and in this way through the practice of the Law of Connection and Relationship, elevate one's consciousness.

Indeed, the study of nature and the physical universe, as well as direct human experience, will assist you to learn another invaluable lesson – as above and within, so below and without. Which, in this instance, means that what you master in your relationship with yourself can then be demonstrated in your relationships with others and with the world as a whole.

Merlin takes another of his periodic pauses. He takes several sips of his herbal brew and then goes within to that space he often visits, leaving Arthur and Aderyn are to allow this information to settle. Then, after several minutes, he opens his eyes and continues.

So the ground of the self is the first and primary learning ground you experience. In this first phase, you are introduced to and have the opportunity to experience and practice many of the dynamics that will ultimately be part of your total human experience.

Do this, and you need not go off and study complex and arcane theories or look very far beyond the scope of what you call ordinary experience to become familiar with the depths and range of the mystery of human existence. Indeed, if you stay present and focus your attention on each moment and observe, with neutrality, your actions and reactions, your concerns and hesitations, as well as your desires and enthusiasms, you will be learning the lexicon of your emotional, intellectual, and spiritual languages. In this way, and only in this way, can you best prepare for the next and equally important stages of relationships with others that will follow.

One can see this by observing or remembering the early life of a child who appears self-focused, even though their sensory experiences allow them to know that a wider world exists.

When one closely observes a child, one discovers that the child tends to relate all things to itself. This allows the child to begin to solidify their foothold in the physical world. So rather than dissuade the child from this stage – and this stage also defines one of the stages every young tribe and community also passes through – it is most prudent to allow the child, and that includes the child within you and in others in the kingdom to fulfill and deepen their engagement and learning in this first stage so that you and they may eventually achieve greater stability and come to know, of your own volition, that the larger outer world is largely a reflection of your inner experience.

As a leader, if you fail to encourage the child within you as well as the children of your kingdom to learn the essential lessons of this first stage lesson, you will ensure that you and they may grow in physical size and gain various capacities, but in many of the most essential and primary ways – emotionally, intellectually, and spiritually – you and they will remain stunted. As a result, the child within you, as well as the children within those you lead will live out their years in this human form in repetitive attempts to fulfill what can no longer be fulfilled because most of us who wear this body are unwilling to keep this early stage of development alive and revisit it often so that we can fulfill its mission and promise.

If, however, you encourage yourself and the children in your kingdom to utilize the first stage of life to learn and practice the lessons for which the next stage of relationship to community is intended, then all will develop a solid relationship with themselves, and this will allow you and them to create relationships of strength and quality with others.

And this relationship with others is the second stage. In it, you and those you lead have the opportunity to understand that a genuine connection and relationship with another is the ground for the deeper practice, experimentation, and understanding of human nature. And this, in turn, will provide you with greater access to the Great Mystery.

For just as in this next stage of our growth, we cannot relate well to others, without having experienced the ground of our primary selves, as a leader, you cannot assist those you lead to prepare for an even wider, deeper, and more positive experience of human consciousness as a tribe or community. Indeed, in forming a connection and relationship with another, exposure to the vast variety of human behaviors is multiplied not just by two, but by an infinite number, and as a result of this multiplication, you and those you will lead will gain exposure and greater mastery over an almost unlimited range of emotions, thoughts, and behaviors.

It is also true that in this second stage of connection and relationship with another, you will, if you practice the art of staying present, learn to identify lessons from the first stage that you or they may not have yet fully mastered or completed. In this way, you and they can use the second stage of connection and relationship to continue to heal some of these incomplete aspects so that in the other stages that follow the second, you will not attempt to make up for what is incomplete and unhealed within yourself by projecting any of your misalignments, and distempers onto the individuals you serve, and the world around you.

So the Law of Relationship and Connection, when well-practiced, will provide you and those you lead with the ability to establish quality relationships first with yourself, then with another, then with your community, and eventually with the Kingdom as a whole, and then with the entire human tribe. And in this larger arena, you and they will then be able to support others in also mastering the Law of Relationship and Connection.

I invite you to remember that if you follow the Natural Flow and its progression and encourage others to do the same; if you remember that one crawls before one walks and walks before one runs, this understanding will, in turn, allow you to demonstrate greater patience with yourself, with process and with others, especially those who are in different stages on this same evolutionary path.

Finally, after you are more practiced in creating positive and constructive relationships with yourself, with another, with the other members of the tribe, and finally with the greater community, you are encouraged to turn more of your attention to deepening your relationship with your inner self and, through this inner self, with the Great Mystery.

This will allow you to harvest the wisdom and experience gained throughout your life, identify aspects of your nature that may still be incomplete or unhealed, and therefore be in a position to do whatever is needed and possible to complete your healing and surrender more and more to the great Mystery itself in the final stage of your life, which of course is not the final stage of existence.

#####

Merlin's Assignment

Through quiet contemplation and careful observation, identify a few lessons that may still be unlearned from your early interaction with the Law of Connection and Relationship. Then make note of the things you can do and practice to better master them in the next stages.

Arthur's Notes Recorded on His Parchment, Later in the Day

Merlin reminded me on this day that as above, so below, as within so without. It is a thing so obvious, and yet it helps me greatly to bring order to my view of the world. However, it also forces me to admit that I, too, often forget this truth as well as the fact that the quality of the relationship I have with others depends on the quality of the relationship I have with myself.

It is certainly true that when I am content and balanced within myself, when I am honest about my limitations and humble over my strengths, I am much more able to be balanced and content in my relationship with others. It is also true that even a small shift in this level of balance and contentment in me soon makes itself apparent in my expressions toward others. Although I must admit that it often takes me a while to become aware of this shift, and, by then, I have often done some harm.

When I reflect on this, I am even more in awe of Merlin. He deals with so many different people under so many different circumstances, not only in what we, ordinary mortals, call the real or seen world, but in his interactions with the unseen world as well.

I can only hope, in the years to come, when I become king, that I will have the courage to continue to deepen my relationship with myself and with the Great Mystery so that I can demonstrate the same kind of wisdom and understanding my teacher does with the many that he serves.

Notes on The Law of Connection and Relationship

Seek first to establish a good and caring relationship with the self. A good and caring relationship with oneself requires observation, honesty, and courage. In the relationship with the self, one gets to practice all of the steps in the human experience. The second necessary stage for the noble leader and the tribe is to establish a true connection with one another. The third and fourth stages involve creating quality connections with one's family and then the greater community. The last stage is to return my focus on deepening the relationship to the Great Mystery.

Chapter Ten - The Law of Compassion & Forgiveness

> **"A ruler should be slow to**
> **punish and swift to reward".**
> –Ovid

Aderyn's Notes

I can tell immediately, as I serve my master his morning brew of herbs, that he is in a quiet, interior place. And so, as I move about to prepare for his next conversation with the young Arthur, I do my best to be, as he had taught me to be at such times, as invisible and silent as possible.

This is one of the many gifts he has shared with me. And the longer I am privileged to be in his service, the more I understand its value. Not only does it allow me to be of greater service to him, but this skill also allows me to move about in the world in a manner that gives me the chance to observe people and events I encounter in ways that others often miss by being so intent on being seen, heard, and acknowledged.

This is a lesson I know Merlin has also shared with my liege lord, Arthur, who has certainly mastered it even more than I have. For I have heard him share with my Master that he can move about among others, he says, especially when he is at court and still retains his freedom to observe and to learn in an unobstructed way. So while I do not yet know the direction this next conversation between Merlin and Arthur will take, I assume that my master's mood is a clue to its possible content and its importance.. And, indeed, as soon as my liege lord arrives, with only a brief greeting and no other preliminaries, Merlin invites us to close our eyes, breathe slowly and deeply, and settle into the silence.

After giving us a longer time than usual to do what he calls, come more fully into presence, Merlin begins speaking in a voice that is soft and measured in that rhythmic tone and cadence I have become accustomed to during these sessions.

Merlin's Lesson

My Son, just as we discovered in the Law of Firsts and again, in the Law of Connection and Relationship, when I advised you of the need and benefit of creating a firm foundation and focusing first on knowing the self before trying to master the world, the same applies in exploring this new Law of Compassion and Forgiveness. I encourage you to learn to develop the capacity to first feel true and deep compassion and forgiveness for yourself, for your strengths and frailties, as well as your uniqueness, your fears, courage, confusions, stumbles, and breakthroughs in all of your undertakings.

This is an essential step on the path to developing true compassion for others, for the many challenges and opportunities life presents, for all other life forms, for the natural environment that is your home, and for all of the levels of the Great Mystery, even those you may not yet understand or comprehend. These things will, however, throughout your life, unfold themselves, sometimes quickly, at others with painstaking slowness, and sometimes not at all. But with each unfolding, the Great Mystery shares more of its secrets. And this, you will find, is an essential step in your emotional and spiritual maturation, which is another prerequisite for success in your role as a noble and enlightened leader.

This counsel is especially true in the case of forgiveness. For only when you have developed a genuine compassion and forgiveness for yourself, particularly for your frailties, and what are commonly called failures, but in reality, you will learn to treasure as genuine gifts, for it is both of these experiences that will teach you to express forgiveness, compassion, and ultimately love for yourself, and especially for those you serve. And forgiveness, compassion, and love are, in the end, my Son, essential keys to living a full, rich, and rewarding existence. An existence in which you eventually make peace with the human condition and better understand how wondrous the many conundrums, challenges, confusions, opportunities, pains, breakdowns, and breakthroughs are.

Merlin pauses here. Studies both Arthur and Aderyn, then takes a drink from his
his cup of herbal brew, then he closes his eyes, and begins to hum a soft and
haunting melody.

Both Arthur and Aderyn also close their eyes, and each is transported to a different inner set of visions in which Merlin is showing them a different healing ritual.

In Arthur's vision, Merlin is teaching him to finish digging a trench just barely wide enough for him to lie down in it and then remain still while Merlin covers him with the earth that he has shoveled into a mound that runs the length of the trench.

Merlin chants in a language that is unknown to Arthur as he does this. And then the moment arrives when all that is left to be covered is his head, and this Arthur knows is the critical part of this initiation. So, although his fear is great, he knows intuitively that he must trust the process and surrender everything to Mother Earth. And it is only when he does so, and begins to feel that he can no longer breathe, that something truly astounding happens. He finds that he is being breathed by a force he cannot describe, and in that instant, any remaining traces of holding on leave him, and he knows that he will not move, regardless of the consequences, until and unless his Master frees him from the earth. And it is then and only then that Merlin removes the earth from his face, and welcomes him joyfully and with pride into the next segment of his journey.

Aderyn, as well, in his vision, is reliving one of his initiations. In his case, he is being asked to administer a healing to a young fawn who had been wounded by a hunter and then left to die. He begins with a chant Merlin has taught him, prepares, and administers a potion made of herbs, flowers he was instructed to collect, as well as sand from the nearby stream bed that he applies to the wound, and then he binds it with a strip from his shirt, all the while chanting an ancient healing chant Merlin has taught him, and sitting with his eyes closed, envisioning in very specific detail, the healing of the fawn.

Merlin returns his presence to the room, clears his throat to announce his return, and then smiles at both of his charges when they open their eyes, and he begins to share the next portion of the Law of Compassion and Forgiveness.

This intimate appreciation and acknowledgment of your humanness, in turn, will invite, inform, and guide you to walk on the path of direct experience and wisdom, and prevent you from walking too exclusively on the path of theory and philosophy, which can too easily become paths on which we hide from what is often a more challenging, direct interaction with life.

While these paths of theory and philosophy are valued by many, they are primarily games of the mind that will ultimately separate you and those you serve from a direct experience of the Natural Flow with all of its grit and tumult. In short, one can hide in thought, but direct engagement and all of the feelings and emotions it prompts, as well as a direct experience of what the majority call the imperfections of life, are where you will find truth.

And this is the ground on which you will develop greater compassion and be able to grant forgiveness which in the end are just forms of love without which you will be a leader in name only and suffer from as great a deficiency as from the failure to remember that to lead is to serve, as from the unwillingness to differentiate between believing and knowing, as from the inability to form true relationships with yourself and others.

And make no mistake, my Son, the pages of history are full of examples of leaders who believed they were above the natural law, and, in the end, their inability to love themselves and others resulted in gross callousness, excessive self-interest, and a host of limiting beliefs that have contributed more pain and suffering than can ever be truly measured.

What else are you, as one who seeks to pursue the path of noble and conscious leadership, advised to learn about compassion and forgiveness? I invite you to understand that while some leaders believe they need to utilize force and power, and instill fear in those they lead, the wise leader knows that these instruments of manipulation and abuse only suffice, and then poorly, and only for a relatively limited period. I also invite you to understand that energy used in this way ultimately exhausts the user as well as greatly limits and retards those he wishes to lead.

Merlin pauses and looks to Aderyn.

Aderyn, tell Arthur about your encounter with the son of the Prince in the Kingdom to the East of Us.

Aderyn

As you may remember, my Liege Lord, my Master, and I traveled there 10 moons ago, at the end of the last summer solstice. When we arrived in the kingdom, the son of the Prince was told to find me a place to sleep in the stables. Merlin had assumed the Prince would understand that I was to be accorded greater deference, but singularly to me was to go along with the Prince's son, I did.

The Prince's son, following his father's lead, assumed that I was not only to sleep in the stables, but that I should be required to clean the stalls. And so he did not ask me, but commanded me to do as I was told. Remembering the look Merlin gave me before I left his presence, I did not object to the young Prince's attempt to order me about. But then the young Prince turned so quickly away that he did not see a shelf that was sticking out from the wall and hit his head with real force against it.

It was enough force to send the young Prince to the ground. I immediately went to him and discovered that he had a large cut on his head and was only partially conscious. Reacting quickly, as my Master had trained me, I located a clean cloth, a pail of warm water, and began ministering to the young prince. After several minutes, he began to regain focus and was embarrassed to find me attending to him.

When I assured him that his wound was not major and that he would be fine if he would allow me to support him, he reluctantly agreed. But it was clear to me that he continued to be embarrassed. What surprised me, however, was what followed. He told me that he'd clearly been trying to impress me with his authority and that he had realized too late that he should have afforded me greater respect. I thanked him for his kindness and, for the first time, I saw that he was, in fact, much younger than he had appeared to me.

And as soon as he understood that I would say nothing to Merlin about his behavior, he relaxed, and over the next hour, we created the basis for a friendship that I am certain will not quickly fade.

Merlin

Nicely told, Aderyn. The kind of misuse of power, and other efforts and practices related to it, that the Prince was demonstrating can be likened to attempts to keep an empty gourd submerged under water. It is a task that requires constant attention and increasing amounts of energy, and even then, with the smallest shift of focus - as occurred when the young man hit his head - the failure to apply precisely the right amount of constant pressure would allow the gourd will slip from one's grasp and pop up to the surface. So it is with true desires and the stumbles and experiences of humanity – they cannot be held down or submerged for long.

So use your unique gifts, true power, and the full majesty and grace of love that allowed you to express compassion, which allowed you and the young Prince to express a nobility and an understanding for each other. This was particularly vital to both of you, and there now, to others who might stumble and stray from the path in what are often called major ways.

Those you lead will also benefit most when you are transparent and do the unexpected by acknowledging that straying and stumbling, although generally perceived by the majority as errors and even crimes that require punishment, are instead necessary and natural stages and prerequisites for gaining experience in life and accumulating wisdom. Indeed, when you openly acknowledge that these seeming departures from the path are not cause for criticism, derision, and abuse, but instead are opportunities for all who wear this human form to pause, identify lessons to be learned, and then discover ways to apply this learning to their future action, you will greatly advance the consciousness of those you serve and, indeed, the consciousness of the time in which you live.

And in cases when straying and stumbling result from inner wounds, the absence of true respect for either oneself, other members of the tribe, or any other form of life, or when an individual or group falls greatly out of alignment with the Great Mystery and does not appear to understand the full consequence of their action, you are advised to remind yourself and those you lead that these states are also part of the process of learning to be human and that the most direct and constructive path forward is the path that leads through compassion, forgiveness and love to healing and realignment with the Natural Flow.

In the most egregious of these instances, however, this does not mean that you, as the one charged with overseeing the collective good, should not sometimes advise and create conditions under which corrective action needs to be taken. But I counsel you to do your best as you take this form of action, to stay in touch with your love, compassion, and forgiveness for yourself and for those you serve. These things will contribute greatly to arriving at the truth and at a fair corrective action and reconciliation. It is this condition that will contribute to greater understanding and mutual ownership by all in the tribe for its well-being.

Also, remember that contributing to this kine of understanding and mutuality, as well as your sharing your joy, enthusiasm, passion, fascination, and your willingness to roll up your sleeves and get involved in the ordinary activities and events that those you lead experience, will ultimately do more to win their hearts and allegiance than attempts to punish or direct them from some false, high perch. Indeed, directing from the heights or the front of the line of engagement may be considered, by some, to be the privilege of the leader, but in the end, these positions do not ultimately inspire and empower others, nor do they demonstrate the courage, commitment, humanity, and equality of a leader to those he leads.

Finally, I invite you to reflect on the lessons identified in the Law of Connection and Relationship, so that you will draw a parallel to the wisdom being offered here. If you spend sufficient time in the realm of cultivating a strong, loving, and compassionate relationship with yourself, then in the realm of relationship with others, and then in your relationship with humankind as a whole, you will continue to gain more understanding about the root of your flaws and be better able to name and explore the lessons you still need to learn. In this way, true compassion, forgiveness, and love for others will become as natural and familiar as each of your breaths.

#####

Merlin's Assignment

I invite you to take some time between this and our next lesson to identify the qualities and characteristics you do not yet have compassion for within yourself. Also, name some things that you have done or now do for which you have not yet forgiven yourself. Lastly, identify at least some things you believe others have done to you for which you have not forgiven them.

Arthur's Notes Recorded on His Parchment, Later in the Day

On this day, Merlin reminded me that true compassion, forgiveness, and love require direct experience, or what he calls maturity. And I am beginning to better understand how true this is. When others share things they have experienced that I have never experienced, I have difficulty understanding the challenges and opportunities these experiences involve. On the other hand, when I have a direct experience similar at least in some ways to those they describe, it is much easier and possible for me to feel these essential things Merlin describes.

This is especially true in regards to forgiveness. When I do something and Merlin does not punish or criticize me, but instead uses it as an opportunity to share an insight or an understanding with me, I am more able to forgive myself and learn from that experience. So it is clear that forgiveness, rather than punishment, is the better way to encourage learning in others.

There are, of course, other times, too many, I must admit, when I am far more critical of myself than others are of me. On these occasions, I find compassion and forgiveness are more difficult to share with myself and, therefore, with others.

This is another of the matters that Merlin says is easier to talk about than to practice. And, the more I reflect upon it, the more I know that when it comes to compassion, forgiveness, and love, I still have much to learn.

Notes on The Law of Compassion and Forgiveness

One must first develop compassion and understanding for oneself before one can express these important qualities to others. One must then seek understanding and acceptance of both the challenges and the opportunities Fate presents. These are prerequisites before the leader can develop genuine compassion and understanding for others. Compassion and understanding for self and others allow the leader to forgive. Demonstrating the true gift and power of compassion and forgiveness in all things and at all times is the true source of power for the leader. Joy, enthusiasm, passion, and the ability to empathize with the lives of those you lead are stepping stones to wisdom.

Chapter Eleven - The Law of Purpose & Meaning

"The purpose of life is not to be happy. It is to be useful, to be honorable, to be compassionate, to have it make some difference that you have lived and lived well."
–Ralph Waldo Emerson

Aderyn's Notes

My master has been away for several days. It is another of his journeys on which he did not ask me to accompany him. And although this is not unusual, as the morning moves toward midday, the time he asked me to set for his next conversation with the younger Arthur, I am surprised that he has not yet returned.

After years of being in his service, I have, of course, learned that Merlin is as unpredictable in his actions as in the many mercurial shifts in his moods and messages, but I still find myself becoming concerned when my liege lord arrives and my master is still not in attendance.

Just as I am about to explain the situation to my liege lord, however, the door to the cottage flies open and Merlin, full of energy and fire, walks in and throws off his great coat, which he always wears when he ventures off on his solitary journeys, even in warmer temperatures. Then he enfolds my liege lord in his bearlike embrace and calls for a cup of his favorite herbs.

He next launches into a most enthusiastic description of a place he has discovered on his return journey, where there are a remarkable number of new buds and shoots of both common as well as rare herbs and plants that he needs for some of his most important healing work.

And, it is clear from the way he describes this location as a very separate domain protected by the spirits whom he refers to as the Elementals, beings he has shared with me on several occasions, who are kin to the Fairies and little people with whom he is often in communication, that he is deeply grateful to have made this discovery.

It is, he says, as if nature creates these sacred domains and keeps them hidden until we are ready or in special need to discover them as another part of the miracle of grace.

As is true of many things, my master does, his enthusiasm is irresistible. I am also reminded that my concern for his well-being is generally misplaced, for he resides in a realm in which he is always surrounded and protected by the Great Mystery. I am reflecting on this fact when I realize that he is about to begin his conversation with my liege lord, and so I have to hurry to take my seat and be ready to transcribe the lesson..

Merlin's Lesson

My Son, as you know, there is no quest greater for the leader or more important to the leader's quest to discover his true purpose in life. There is also no quest more demanding, more necessary, and ennobling for a leader than to be sure that this purpose is in harmony and alignment with the Great

Mystery.

Yes, there is a most important thing about purpose. It requires surrender to the process, genuine inquiry, and discovery rather than attempts to achieve it by force of will. The same is true regarding the sense of meaning associated with purpose. It is not separate from one's true path, but rather it emerges naturally from purpose if one pays close attention. In this way, and only in this way, can you or anyone who wishes to lead play their part in ensuring the greater good.

To uncover both purpose and meaning, I encourage you to devote sufficient time and have the requisite courage to journey with enthusiasm in both the inner and outer dimensions. I also encourage you to be willing to cross into territory often discouraged and sometimes even forbidden by those who champion the safety of the known, and the comfort of the habitual and the logical.

Yes, I invite you to be willing to experience the discomfort of confusion and the vagaries of doubt that will most assuredly arise whenever you turn away from the known and from those who would keep you confined within it. You would also be wise to remember that their efforts, although seemingly well-intentioned, will not contribute to your well-being and growth as much as they will protect them from having to make their journey of discovery into this most mysterious and challenging territory.

I also invite you to accept the restlessness that occurs when unanswered questions arise from your encounters with the unknown, and from your interactions with the obstacles and resistances that arise when you leave the protection of the familiar and enter more deeply into the Great Mystery. Also, remember that when you journey beyond the places on the path where others have stopped, you will likely find that you travel these portions of the journey alone, and as a scout, adventurer, and path-finder for those who are not yet able or who are too timid to ever make their journey. So be mindful and appreciate both the honor and the responsibility of these steps that you will take beyond the boundary of the known and to the places you must visit in your quest if you are committed to being a noble and conscious leader.

I advise you to practice the essential gift of not just looking, but seeing; not just listening, but hearing; not just thinking, but comprehending, and, of particular import, not just feeling but learning to surrender to following the wisdom of your heart.

Merlin pauses as he has periodically in all of the sessions to date, when he believes
the ground covered is important enough to warrant taking the time to integrate it.
So he closes his eyes and turns his attention inward.

As both Arthur and Aderyn reflect on what has been said, each, in their way, focuses on a specific moment when the topic of purpose and meaning surfaced in a very meaningful way. For Arthur, it was a conversation that he had with Guinevere. They had taken a ride up to an overlook in the surrounding hills that they both considered to be a special place. And once there, these two unique young people who would one day play a major role not only in each other's lives, but in the history of their time shared some secrets they had never before told each other.

During Adeyn's reflections, he returns to a conversation he had had several years ago with Merlin, during which the wizard had challenged him to define an ideal day in the life he wanted to live. He had trouble that day, looking into the eyes of his master and telling him that the day he was living was a clear example of what he envisioned to be the kind of life of genuine purpose and meaning he wanted to live.

Merlin returns from his inner journey.

These are but some of the things I encourage you to do if you hope to discover your authentic meaning and purpose and achieve things of lasting value in utilizing it. And, this does not yet speak adequately of the many moments along the way when your resolve will be tested beyond levels that you believe you can endure. Moments in which your endurance and your faith in the value of your quest will, most certainly, be challenged by the myriad of illusions, phantoms, and doubts of different shapes and consequences that will arise and must be identified, addressed, and ultimately either defeated or befriended along the way. This, my Son, is the path that you will be asked to travel if you truly wish to uncover and confirm your meaning and purpose and to use it to serve the Great Mystery.

So be clear, your quest for purpose and meaning will not be an easy one, but if you remain open and receptive there will come times when the Great Mystery will, of its own volition, introduce you to allies, offer unexpected resources, and lift at least a portion of the veil long enough to rekindle your sense of hope, stimulate your courage and renew your willingness to proceed. It is these and other precious gifts and discoveries that will support you as you continue on your journey with an innocent heart and a true sense of commitment.

And, these gifts and unexpected aids, when accepted, will also often prove to be precisely what is needed to re-ignite your passion, and re-stimulate your intention long enough to allow you to ultimately, one step forward, one breath, one moment at a time, move forward. They will also help you to win the prize of uncovering that which has been held within your deeper and truer self from the beginning.

Following this path of purpose and meaning, you will eventually come to more fully comprehend more of the Great Mystery and celebrate and honor the role you have agreed to play. It is. My Son, a commitment you made long before assuming this physical form and entering the unfolding drama of life in this dimension. In this way, and only in this way, will you know that you have found what is authentically yours, and then you will require courage and persistence to remain true to the deepest and truest values, to continue to surrender more fully, and to accept the guidance you will require to take every essential next step.

The alternative, for those like you, my Son, of whom much will be asked, is to refuse to undertake the quest to discover your true purpose and meaning. However, be clear that you will then be like a boat without a rudder. You will wander aimlessly and at the mercy of every changing wind and current of chance. And I do not say this to force your hand, as they say. Only to let you know the true cost of not leaving behind the comfort of the known to go in search of your rightful place in the Great Mystery, you, like the vast majority of those you see moving about the kingdom and the greater world when you begin to travel within it, will be required to accept what I can only call a life of regret and sadness. As a result, you will not only have difficulty arriving at your desired port of call, but you will have forfeited your opportunity to add your original and unique song in the symphony that is the Great Mystery.

By comparison, if you follow your heart and go in quest to uncover and stay true to your purpose and meaning, you will eventually find that your hand is strongly positioned on the tiller and you will be able to navigate your way out of the thickest of fogs and sail beyond the most turbulent stretches of the sea and into the sunlight and the winds of good grace.

And this is not to make that claim that your life will be easy, without pain and suffering, and the requirement to ultimately surrender all that you possess, but what you will experience is a level of wonder, a true understanding of audacity, and the knowledge that you are and will fulfill your destiny. So look not to other beings but to the wisdom of nature and other life forms, as well as to the allies who always wait in silence within you for an invitation to contribute. Remember that you will appear many times to be alone on your journey, there will come a day when you understand that you are always protected and that there will always be unseen helpers and allies all around you, and all you need do is remain true to your quest and you retain the capacity to ask for their support with humility, integrity, and a true and open heart.

Above all, remember to commit and immerse yourself fully in each task with that which we have spoken of previously, called fascination. For this is a gift of great consequence. Remember that your first and only priority is to serve, and that the entire cosmos is an interrelated and interdependent creation. Remember, these things will make your path more possible and passable, even if it will most likely not be said that it is easy.

But if you have the discipline and courage to forgo the seduction of false shortcuts, you are mindful to avoid using manipulation and avoid the temptation to substitute power for wisdom and sufficiency for material reward. If you remember that force is never as effective as patience and working with the flow, and with present-moment awareness is far more valuable than the bluster and fury of trying to recreate the past or artificially create the future, and that listening to the guidance of the heart will always the key to truth, these practices will allow you to form an unbreakable alliance with the Great Mystery and in this way, you will be aided in accomplishing that which is in the best and highest good for yourself as well as for those you serve.

Arthur, I share today's assignment, and before we conclude. I wonder if you would be so kind as to share one of the characteristics or qualities about yourself you have not yet had the compassion to forgive or accept.

Arthur Is Slow To Respond

Merlin, I regret that there are a number of characteristics that I demonstrate that I do not yet have either the courage or the compassion to forgive or accept. But one that is most troubling is my doubt about whether I am truly suited to be king.

Merlin Smiles and Then Proceeds To Give Arthur His Next Assignment
#####

Merlin's Assignment

Observe yourself as you make your passage from first light to darkness each day and determine if what you think, say, and do aligns with your purpose. Also, ask yourself if these things bring greater or less meaning to you and to those you serve.

Arthur's Notes Recorded on His Parchment, Later in the Day

Merlin spoke on this day of purpose. It is a thing I am familiar with. I was already aware of having a purpose when my father first invited Merlin to be my primary guardian and teacher. In fact, except for a few times, the most recent being a year or so ago, when I rebelled against the idea of one day becoming king, I have been fortunate to know that I am called and guided by something greater than myself. Something Merlin often reminds me of when I do not demonstrate the level of commitment in the tasks and actions I have agreed to do is the reason I have taken on this human form.

There are others I know who also know their purpose. And number this includes people at both ends of what Merlin calls the path of life. Those, like me, who have been blessed, as Merlin often reminds me, with the grace that has been showered upon us. But strangely, this also holds for the many who are less fortunate and who spend the majority of their lives toiling from dawn to dusk doing what they must to survive. So, it seems people in both of these groups know their purpose.

However, it appears that many exist on the road between these two groups. They are those Merlin refers to as being in the middle. They do not have the privileges of those who surround my father, the king, nor do they have to toil from dusk to dawn. As a result, they do not seem to be called by some larger purpose. Indeed, in many instances, they seem to be separated from the understanding that they must search for it.

On the question of meaning, however, at least based on Merlin's words, it seems to be something different from purpose. And while he tells me that one finds meaning when they follow their purpose, it is a thing I have some questions about. What does one do when they do not find meaning in what one does? And how does one find meaning in something they consider usual and ordinary and not necessarily connected to their purpose?

Another question that troubles me is how I, as a leader, can support others in finding greater purpose and meaning, especially if, at the same time, part of my task is to require them to do what is necessary to maintain and preserve the kingdom through the performance of what is ordinary.

Yes, I have many questions on the Law of Purpose and Meaning, and no doubt when I ask Merlin about some of these, he will remind me that questions are among our most important allies. For when they are well asked and diligently pursued, they do unlock more of The Great Mystery.

Notes on The Law of Purpose and Meaning

There is no quest more important than the quest to discover one's purpose.

Without true meaning and purpose, the leader and those he leads are like boats without rudders. To accomplish one's quest for meaning and purpose, one must journey in both the inner and outer dimensions. Patience, curiosity, wonder, audacity, courage, and surrender are essential qualities to practice on the path. Stay true to the quest, and the Great Mystery will offer allies and support. Stay true to the quest, and the leader will find the way out of the densest fog and into the sunlight.

Chapter Twelve - The Law of Aligned Values

"Your beliefs become your thoughts,
Your thoughts become your words,
Your words become your actions,
Your actions become your habits,
Your habits become your values,
Your values become your destiny."
–Mahatma Gandhi

Adreryn's Notes

A brilliant sun, a mild wind, and very comfortable temperatures offer additional signals of Spring's arrival. They are signs that many in the kingdom have been patiently awaiting. And, while most understand that there will, in all likelihood, be other days ahead when rain and some chill will mark this transition between winter and summer, everyone, including my master and his student, seems intent on celebrating the beauty of this day.

So I add the pelts made from the skin of rabbits, whom my Master has instructed me to always honor for their sacrifice in providing food to sustain us, and comfort to the chairs that will provide Merlin and my liege lord with some warmth when the afternoon sun slides behind the surrounding hills and the chill returns. Both then settle into their respective places on the rise adjacent to the cottage. However, before my master begins the next lesson, he questions my liege lord about his progress on his most recent assignments.

As I listen to Arthur share his experience and await the start of the session, I am aware that the joy of Spring that has called us outdoors has also stimulated harmonies in the songs of the birds and in the colors visible in the fields around us that are growing more alive each day. Fresh buds and new leaves are beginning to adorn the trees, and hope is present in the tender shoots that are poking their way up among the scattered leaves and ground cover. This wonder is also apparent in the spirit that seems to animate the conversation between my liege lord and my master, which has set the stage for Merlin's calling us into the quiet.

Merlin's Lesson

My Son, much as is the case on this day, when, after the long period of confinement within our Winter dwellings, we emerge to this celebration of beauty that delights our senses with its many sights, sounds, and scents, our focus encompasses this multitude and helps expand and sharpen the scope of our awareness. It also provides us with an overview and a worthy perspective, both of which are precious gifts.

It is also true, however, that a multiple focus can sometimes be distracting and prevent us from experiencing a deeper observation and engagement in any one of the details that present themselves. In many ways, this can be likened to standing on both a wooden pier and a boat at the same time. While it offers us different choices and can be an interesting experience, if one wants to maintain balance and move along on their journey, a moment will arrive when it will be necessary to choose where to place their full weight and attention.

I believe this is an important lesson for everyone and, most especially for you, if you wish to inspire and empower those you serve and do not wish to find your choice of the shore or the boat taken from you when the space between them increases to the point that you are about to fall into the water that lies between them.

This applies to the positions or stands you will be called upon to take, on matters of principle, issues of policy and governance, and core beliefs held by both you and those you lead.

Although those who consider themselves adept in the ways of the world suggest that focusing on multiple objects and subjects and multiple activities and advancing multiple values and principles is necessary and important, the wisdom of the sages suggests caution.

Eventually, even those capable of dividing their attention and focusing on multiple things must arrive at the time when they must let go of multiple positions. The same is true of those moments when one must stop evaluating options or various positions and make a decision in favor of one or the other. For if one varies their stand on values and principles and attempts to defend multiple positions at the same time, especially if one is a leader, they will eventually find themselves suspended in the space between these principles with ever-diminishing forces and without the capacity to focus on one of them. As a result, little of genuine value is gained, and in many instances, the well-being of the leader and that of those they lead can be put at risk.

This is not to say that maintaining a multiple focus or holding more than one position initially when exploring and investigating something in the preliminary stages is a bad thing. However, once this initial stage has passed, and once you have explored and investigated the available options, collected preliminary information, consulted both internal and external sources of knowledge, and arrived at an initial evaluation of the value of one choice or position over that, I advise you to center yourself and then proceed accordingly in establishing a firm stance or point of attention on your choice.

I caution you, however, that if it becomes apparent, at a later point in time, and as a result of new or additional information coming to light, your original decision or position appears too limited or inappropriate, I encourage you to alter your course and to do so without apology or concern, but with transparency. For just as the natural order of things is change, so should you, as a leader, be willing to change.

Merlin pauses to see if either Arthur or Aderyn has a question or comment; they are moved to ask or add. Aderyn is still capturing his notes on the lesson, but Arthur has been activated by something Merlin has said.

Arthur

I am often accused by my father, the king, of procrastinating too much, but from my perspective, I believe he is too quick to reach a decision, and that as a result, some of his decisions often require reversal.

Merlin

You, My Son, and your father, the King, are cut from different cloths. This does not mean that one of you is more correct than the other. Only that you have different ways of viewing and responding to an event or a person.

If I might suggest an experiment for your edification. The next time you are asked to share your perspective on a topic or person, try changing your traditional process and see if you can find any benefit or advantage. And when you then return to your traditional process, measure that experience.

Merlin adjusts his position in his chair, takes a sip of his herbal brew

and allows his hands to invite both young men's attention

It is also true, and of particular consequence for you and others called upon to lead, to be sure that positions you take on matters of principle, issues of policy and governance, and core beliefs should remain consistent and aligned with your values as long as you are committed to these values. Again, this does not mean that you should not alter your position on all or any of these things – only that as long as you hold these values to be true, you should model and support them to the best of your ability in your words and actions.

I offer, here, another caution of great import. Like a father who wishes to teach his children well, I strongly advise you to avoid the tendency to promote one set of core values and matters of consequence to the children of your tribe and demand their adherence to and practice of them while, at the same time, violating them in the conduct of your affairs. Nor should you, if and when you discover additional or new information that shifts your perspectives, continue to insist on strict adherence by those you lead to the previously held values and principles simply because such adherence is more convenient for you.

In this way, your alignment will not become rigid, only consistent. For indeed, values and principles, like beliefs, are intended to be temporary guidelines that can assist you as well as those you lead to assemble, organize, and direct attention and resources for the accomplishment of goals that are for the best and highest good at a particular time or place along the path of daily life. As such, these beliefs should only be held by you or those you lead until new perspectives and understandings allow you and those you lead to elevate their consciousness and articulate their new core values.

#####

Merlin's Assignment

I ask you to consider how you come to know when you have collected sufficient information on a given course of action or a specific belief, even a long-standing one, to make a decision, and how you will know when it may be time to change course. And by what measure or standards will you determine if your words and actions are in alignment with your values and beliefs?

Arthur's Notes Recorded on His Parchment, Later in the Day

It has not been an easy time for me. Some of my other duties have not gone as well as my involvement in these lessons on leadership and governance. I recognize that I have not felt the same commitment to their execution, and as a result, to the quality of my performance. Merlin says this is because I have an aptitude for these new topics, and an aversion and avoidance, he adds quickly and with a laugh, to some of the others.

Still, if I am to be a noble and wise king, I do not believe I should make such distinctions between this lesson or task or that task. Just as I should not make distinctions between one person and another.

Merlin says that it will be of great importance to me to learn to value all things equally, even if I have a preference for one over another. He also laughs, however, when I tell him I find this hard to do. "Who has ever made the claim," he asks in that deep and imposing voice, "that one's path is supposed to be easy, or that the search for alignment between one's actions and one's values is a simple matter?"

And I cannot dispute the truth of Merlin's words. And if this alignment were an easy thing to accomplish, many of us would be leading more exemplary lives.

Notes on The Law of Aligned Values

Focus one's attention on multiple goals initially until one has determined their viability. Once a goal is validated, commit sufficient attention and resources to its achievement. In matters of principle, issues of policy, governance, and core beliefs, consistency of commitment is essential. When new information and experience suggest new principles, policies, governance, and core beliefs, adopt them with trust and without hesitation. Alignment with principles, policies, governance, and core beliefs is essential for the leader as it is for those he leads. Alignment is consistent, but it is not rigid.

Chapter Thirteen - The Law of Natural Flow

"Life is a series of natural and spontaneous changes
Don't resist them; that only creates sorrow.
Let reality be reality. Let things flow naturally
Forward in whatever way they like."
Lao Tzu

Aderyn's Notes

Having been away for an extended journey to the South to attend a gathering of
leaders from various portions of the realm with his father, my liege lord Arthur
has returned, and like the Spring, now in full and resplendent blossom, he has
much to share and with great enthusiasm about some of the ways the Laws of
Noble Leadership and Conscious Governance that have been imparted to him to
date by my master were both visible and in many other instances sadly lacking
among the leaders present.

So as he and my master sit on the balcony of the Watch Tower that provides an
expansive view of the landscape, he shares some of these observations and answers
questions posed by my master.

When it becomes apparent that my liege lord seems to have shared the most essential things he experienced on his journey, my master, as is his custom, invites us to close our eyes, breathe deeply, and enter the silence so that we will be better able to both hear and listen to the subject he is now ready to share.

Merlin's Lesson

My Son, as you have observed during your travels, there are some leaders in this time, and I assure you that there will be many more in the times ahead, who will insist that the Laws of Man have been handed down to them directly from the Gods, and therefore they pretend that they are original and truer than anything else. I encourage you, however, to remember that it is the Law of Natural Flow emanating directly from the Great Mystery that always has been and will always be the primary law.

So, always remain faithful to your study of the natural flow. In this way so you will come to know even more of its variations, both subtle and those that are more pronounced, its vagaries and conundrums, its sudden and dramatic shifts, and its cycles, both short and long in duration, that directly impact life in these times.

Then look for ways to apply these lessons learned through your observations, particularly when it comes to the rhythms, harmonies, and the principles that underlie the natural flow as they apply to the affairs of men. I believe you will find this much more valuable than following the suggestions made by others who attempt to devise new and artificial rhythms and harmonies to explain or govern the affairs of men, affairs that too often are designed to abuse, resist, contradict, and/or subvert the Natural Law.

If you follow the natural flow, you will lead with dignity, decency, and, ultimately, with genuine consciousness and great success – success being defined as the best and highest good of the greatest number. If, on the other hand, you attempt to contradict these natural laws, you can be certain that pain and sorrow for yourself and those you lead will eventually result.

The Law of Natural Flow, for example, does not favor straight lines, rigid forms, and inflexible beliefs or practices. These are among the illusions that arise from the forced creations, aberrations, and mental constructs of man. Instead, the Law of Natural Flow aligns with and discloses aspects of the Greater Mystery and celebrates ambiguity, irregularity, variation, flexibility, and uniqueness. The Law of Natural Flow honors and demonstrates constant change and not the illusion of the status quo.

Another aspect of the Law of Natural Flow that I encourage you to pay close attention to as you go about the conduct of your daily affairs is the awareness that 'enough declares itself, a subject we will explore more fully in a future lesson.

Yes, my Son, if you are wise, patient, and committed to supporting the best and highest good for yourself and those you serve, you will come to understand that there is great, perfect, and long-term balance within the Great Mystery. While this balance may not be apparent to those who lack patience, may not serve the self-focused, nor advance the objectives of those who see control by the few over the many, I encourage you not to concern yourself with their interests.

Yes, the balance inherent in the Law of Natural Flow may not be discernible to those anxious for a specific result, especially a specific result that is designed to serve their pre-defined objectives. So if you remember the Law of Perspective, and remember that the Great Mystery has evolved over countless eons, through periods of calm and of tumult, and that it offers great beauty and grandeur, magnificence and abundance, and things that are often misperceived or abused by those who lack the gift of perspective, you will not lose your way or lead your people in errant directions.

Merlin pauses here and looks to Arthur.

Arthur, you and I have often talked about some of the ways that man can protect and preserve the Natural Flow.

Arthur

You have told me that man can support the Natural Flow by encouraging the alternation of the pathways taken to prevent excessive use of any route. Vary the use of fields for the grazing animals and the growing of crops not to deplete them; support the cycles of the growth of various crops to increase the stability and nourishment of the land. Encourage others to alternate the location of the cutting of woodlands so that re-growth is more possible; see to it that the gathering of stones does not deplete one area so that the land becomes subject to erosion. Also, do all that we can to be sure the areas where we fish and hunt are used in alternating rhythm and cycles to allow for the replenishment of the supply of food that will sustain you and your people.

Merlin smiles

Yes, my Son, if we are wise, we will apply these lessons of the Law of Natural Flow in the pursuit of all tasks, as well as in an effective and disciplined use of all resources, and, above all, in the care, support, and nourishment of those you lead.

Remember that true abundance and sustenance cannot come if resources are abused or if there is rapid accumulation of material wealth by the few in the pursuit of short-term goals and for limited, short-term perspectives. Instead, always hold close to the understanding that true abundance issues from the ability to understand, honor, celebrate, and protect the cycles of harvesting and planting, and from the regeneration and careful management of resources that are the gifts of the Great Mystery.

Remember that the Law of Natural Flow is available everywhere and at all times for our study and practice. This is true and faithful advice. Only when greed and gluttony, and the lust for power and domination of the few over the many, gain the upper hand does the leader lose his way, and calamities ensue.

Remember as well that if it is possible for a stream to find its way through and around seemingly insurmountable obstacles; if a stone can lie buried beneath the earth's surface for eons under intense pressure and then emerge as something of great beauty and value; if a single seed, shed as fruit from a tree, can ultimately find its true place in the earth and grow to be a companion and sometimes an even a protector of the living thing from which it sprang; if a bird can leave in one season, travel countless hectares and return to the very same location and at the very same time year after year again and again, then it should be equally possible for those of us who wear this human form and who call ourselves leaders play a vital part in protecting the natural flow and in teaching those we lead to do the same.

The Great Mystery, seemingly divided and manifesting in a myriad of shapes and forms, invests the same wisdom into every part of the whole. It should, indeed, be possible for each of us, and most especially for leaders charged with ensuring the greatest good of the greatest number, to invest the time and the energy to observe the natural flow and gain from this observation as well as from enough direct experimentation with the natural world, the wisdom to guide the affairs of man.

In this way, you and those who lead will come to remember: as above, so below; as within, so without. You will remember that each aspect of the Great Mystery manifesting in the physical world is precious. No one aspect is less valuable. The earth, sky, water, fire, and wind are all living entities. Even those objects and elements that may appear solid and seemingly inanimate to the majority of us are filled with the same precious energy that infuses you and me, and Aderyn ran. Every single object that shares this environment with us is a vital part of the Great Mystery and deserves to be honored and well-used.

These are among the many gifts and lessons available to you through the close observation and study of The Law of Natural Flow.

#####

Merlin's Assignment

Since the Law of Natural Flow involves constant change and ambiguity, I ask you to reflect on how you best learn to stay connected to the one constant that lies beneath all that changes. How do you remember it and locate it when you need to consult with it? And how do you test every decision you make to discover if you are in or out of alignment with the natural flow?

Arthur's Notes Recorded on His Parchment, Later in the Day

How easy and simple my teacher makes the Law of Natural Flow appear. And after these years of being in his presence, I know he speaks the truth. But, at the same time, I also know I do not always practice this law, nor do I see it practiced by many in our realm.

While in some instances, fields are allowed to renew and hunting grounds and streams and rivers are allowed time to replenish, it is also true that many in the realm act with what my teacher calls only self-interest, and as a result, they do not honor this law.

There are other ways people do not honor this law. Instead, like a stream that is present and easy to follow at one moment and then disappears into a hillside or beneath a pile of boulders in the next, many do not trust the Natural Flow when it is not immediately visible. They also hunt in areas where hunting is not allowed and continue to seed and harvest fields again and again without allowing them time to renew before doing so.

So I wonder how to convince them of the importance of this law when it is my turn to lead, especially if I do not always demonstrate the law and its benefits myself. And if what Merlin said this day is true, that the Law of the Natural Flow is unchanging, how do I convince my people to sacrifice something on one day, if they cannot yet see how they will benefit from this sacrifice on some future day?

Notes on The Law of The Natural Flow

The Law of Natural Flow always has been and always will be the primary law. The leader is advised to study nature and to come to know its variations, both subtle and major. The Law of Natural flow does not value straight lines, rigid forms, and absolutes. The Great Mystery demonstrates great and noble balance, flexibility, and true abundance. The Law of Natural Flow speaks to alternation in the use of natural resources as the key to their preservation. The Law of Natural Flow is always available for study and practice by those who lead.

Chapter Fourteen - The Law of No Harm

"Non-violence is the greatest force at the disposal of mankind.
It is mightier than the mightiest weapon of destruction devised
by the ingenuity of man."
−Mahatma Gandhi

Aderyn's Notes

For a reason I cannot, at first, discover, my master does not wait the normal amount of time between sessions before asking me to invite my liege lord to join him for their next conversation.

It is only when Arthur arrives and the conversation begins that I learn that my master has been invited to another kingdom to attend a gathering of others who belong to the brotherhood of practitioners of what those of us who are less gifted refer to as the healing and magic arts.

To my surprise, I also learn that I am to accompany him, a privilege that has never before been accorded me for a gathering of this magnitude. And, as a result, it takes me a little while and several motivating looks from my master to return my

attention to the present moment and to my task of being prepared to accurately
capture the essence of the new lesson he is about those share with young Arthur.

Merlin's Lesson

My Son, many who lead, especially those who are impatient and arrogant and
who believe they are superior to those they lead, and are driven to achieve
goals they deem of paramount importance and that advance their personal
needs far more than the goals of those they serve, do this without consulting
the Oracle of the Greater Good.

Generally aggressive, bold, they are generally wrongly convinced of their
special skills and rights, a combination of qualities they believe justifies them
to follow routes that arise from the mind and reason, and not from the heart,
and are revealed to them by spirit. As a result, these routes they follow often
prove circuitous and neither constructive for those they lead, nor ultimately,
for themselves..

So, for you and others who aspire to lead with nobility and greater consciousness. I suggest you take great care in separating yourselves from those who
lead with arrogance and impatience. I suggest you befriend the Oracle of the
Greater Good and always consult it as part of your process. Also, take the
time to identify the value and long-term consequences of each of the goals
you wish to pursue on behalf of those you lead, test the strategies you your
are inclined to take in achieving them, before you commit major resources
to their accomplishment, and most particularly, experiment with various
practices you can employ that will enlist rather than force or demand the
support of others.

You see, My Son, impatient, arrogant, and less-skilled leaders, and there are
certainly many of these who are rising to their positions in this time. Many,
as we have discussed, have not been required to test their mettle in the fires
of true initiation. Others who rise by deception, cunning, manipulation, and

often by committing inhuman crimes against their brethren, and fail to place sufficient value on the impact the goals they are inclined to pursue will have on those they lead, on Natural Law, and in disregard for the Great Mystery, they violate the Law of No Harm.

Indeed, many of these leaders are too focused on producing short-term results that they believe demonstrate their competence and superiority, thereby increasing their gluttony and desire for power and domination over those they lead. In this way, they fail in their endeavors and end up bringing great confusion and suffering to others.

This is both unfortunate and unnecessary. Unfortunate because when they focus so exclusively on their accomplishments and benefits and on what they mistakenly view as their just rewards for their actions, they attempt to perform an impossible feat. They attempt to divide that which is indivisible and to conquer that which is only achieved by surrender and true service to the greater good.

This type of leader, in considering these efforts justified and these temporal accomplishments of values, turns the journey of life into a perpetual contest and, in this way, violates the Law of No Harm. Yes, My Son, this type of leader who mistakenly walks on this errant path commits himself to a perpetual struggle, fails to benefit from collaboration and cooperation with others, forfeits genuine accomplishment for the illusion of power, which is always fleeting, empty of real satisfaction and joy, and always ends up missing the mark.

Merlin pauses here to track the inner paths being taken by both his student and his scribe, who are attempting to integrate this material. Knowing the true implications of the tenets of this Law of No Harm, and recognizing how different and seemingly contrary they may appear to the demands of this time, when there are many early signs of turmoil brewing in the kingdom, and even greater signs in other kingdoms in the world at large. Signs that prompt far too many leaders, even Arthur's father, who, for the most part, has been a good and wise king, to begin to impose more restrictive edicts and more severe forms of punishment.

And this is precisely the topic that has Arthur's attention as he reflects on several recent events when he has witnessed his father in the open council sessions that have, for as long as Arthur can remember, marked his father's reign as open and without turmoil, become angry and dismissive.

On one such occasion, after the villagers had departed, his father began a conversation with his most trusted advisors, and Arthur was surprised to hear comments from the king and several others that were unlike any he had ever heard before.

And when he later spoke to his father about his concerns and mentioned his confusion, his father, to his surprise and for the first time in memory, treated him more like a boy than the man he believed he was becoming.

It was a very troubling experience for him, but until Merlin began sharing tenets of the Law of No Harm, he had not admitted how much that exchange with his ather impacted him. As he briefly reflects on the years he has spent studying with Merlin, he begins to realize that he has always believed that the counsel and recommendations made by his teacher were intended to be cautionary tales about other leaders and other kingdoms.

As he sits there in Merlin's cottage, however, the future king begins to glimpse a very different possibility, and this possibility leaves him both confused and not a little adrift.

Merlin, for his part, having been following Arthur's inner process, is aware that a consequential and yet inevitable moment has arrived. But he also realizes this i not a time to try to address all of the implications.

When Merlin turns his attention to Aderyn, it is clear that without knowing the full cause, he, too, is also aware that something of major consequence has just occurred in this space.. So Merlin nods in encouragement of awareness and then clears his throat and begins to speak again.

Merlin

What is the mark I referred to earlier? Always advance the greater good for the greatest number. Always serve the well-being of those they serve. Always elevate their consciousness and that of their people. And always empower them to live the lives they were born to live.

These things cannot be achieved when a leader focuses too exclusively on personal goals, nor if he is moved to respond to things he does not yet understand out of fear and tries to impose his will on his subjects. Nor can the greater good be achieved when a leader decides some of these individuals in his kingdom are superior and therefore assigns others to lower levels, a division that generally allows those who lead to treat those they place lower on their arbitrary scale as expendable, and as fodder to be used as pawns who can be sacrificed at will. These actions speak to a flagrant lack of alignment with the Great Mystery.

Instead, to advance the greater good of the greatest number, I invite you to remember that all living forms are interconnected, all exist by the grace of the Great Mystery, and, therefore, all are equally entitled to the gifts bestowed by the natural flow. So, when you consider whether or not leadership is truly your path and whether or not you have the requisite strength of character and depth of values to lead with nobility and consciousness, I invite you to keep this fundamental Law of No Harm close in your heart.

In formulating new laws, evaluating and redefining ones that are already in place, a thing I heartily recommend you do regularly, especially if you wish to set new norms and policies; and in dealing with those who you may consider adversaries, in adjudicating disputes between individuals or actions within the kingdom or between this kingdom and another, if your decision or action leaves some with what they desire or require and others in substantial lack then know that you are attempting to distort the Natural Flow.

Therefore, never seek more than you need. Never take from another that which they need for their well-being. Indeed, never take something from another unless you can replace it with something of at least equal or greater value. Never leave another in distress if there is something you can do to contribute to the alleviation of their distress. Never elevate yourself at the cost of another. Never advance your position through the suppression or the distortion of truth, the manipulation of others for your gain, or the express or cause violence to be administered to achieve your aim.

In short, My Son, as a noble leader, always seeks to serve through equity, collaboration, cooperation, and just sharing. Always do what is possible to leave each being, each object, and circumstance you encounter better off than when you first encounter them. And in this way, always remember that you are a servant of the Great Mystery and a practitioner of the Law of No Harm.
#####

Merlin's Assignment

In a world in which you will constantly be asked to decide between one cause and another, one direction to be taken vs another, or a claim made by this individual or group against another, I invite you to begin considering how you can best decide in favor of one without doing great harm to another. Or if harm is done or appears to be done, how might you mitigate this harm for the greater good? And above all, I ask you to consider the full consequences and challenges you will accept when you take on the mantle of the king in this time of turbulence on which we are embarking.

Arthur's Notes Recorded on His Parchment, Later in the Day

Of all of the things my teacher has instructed me to practice, the Law of No Harm seems to be one of the most difficult, especially in some of the areas Merlin spoke about. Such as the formulation of new laws, the making peace with adversaries, or the quieting of disputes between individuals or factions

While I can see how this law might sometimes be employed, when I look at the way things occur in the natural flow. When some in the kingdom are lost to disease and others live; when animals in a herd are slaughtered or lost and others allowed to survive; when high winds or floods destroy some dwellings or crops or sections of the forest and others remain untouched; when one child in a family is visited by death while his sibling remains unharmed, how does one explain this seeming randomness of the natural flow and practice the Law of No Harm?

And even in those matters that will fall within my duties and on which I will someday be asked to make decisions - decisions between the claims made by two individuals who appear to have equal grievance or equal grounding for their position; questions regarding the nature of punishment for crimes committed by one against another or against many that appear, at first to be without cause, but upon closer examination disclose a misalignment or some undiscovered prior offense? How can I be certain that in choosing one course of action, one punishment over another, I will be doing right and not harming someone, because I do not understand the root or the cause of their action?

At this moment, it seems an almost impossible task. And yet, as I listened to Merlin speak on this law today, I thought I glimpsed, in the space that followed some of his words, a path that I might take, different than the one I sense my father may be considering, that involves what I hold in my heart when I am the one who must make a decision rather than in the decision itself. Perhaps if I am in balance and open to the truth, and my intention is pure and to be of genuine service, I will find my way to do what I must to the best of my ability.

As I ponder these significant questions, I am aware that this is another matter that requires greater consideration and much more conversation with my teacher. And I sense it will be among those questions, as Merlin often tells me, that are best answered by my using excellence and not perfection as the measure of success.

I also realized today, that my path to noble leadership may well put me on a collision course, not only with others in this time who are not committed to fulfilling their role as servants of the greater good, but even with my father, who I pray, with all my heart, will return to a higher path before it is too late and not willingly include himself with the many that Merlin has described as having lost their way.

Notes on The Law of No Harm

Temper impatience with the willingness to consult the Oracle of the Greater Good. Always identify both the value and long-term consequences of the goals, strategies, and practices. Leaders committed only to short-term results generally fail. The goal of value is always that which best serves the greater good. The goal is to empower and elevate the consciousness of those one leads. The ultimate goal is to support others to live the lives they were born to live.

Chapter Fifteen - The Law of Enough

"Enough declares itself."
Ancient Proverb

Aderyn's Notes

The full warmth and radiance of Summer are now present in our valley when my master and I return from our journey. And I must say that although I was aware that much was transpiring during our time away and that I had been exposed to things that had altered me in ways I am not yet even able to describe, it is only when we enter the glen and I see the cottage that I am privileged to share with my master, that I begin to recognize how much I value my home here and that this is just one of the many differences in perspective my travels have granted me.

The harmony of the landscape, the quiet sense of beauty, and all that is familiar about my life here bring up within me a sense of deep gratitude. And, I must also admit that I feel a degree of sadness as well. For I now understand that although I have accompanied my master on short trips before and witnessed other customs and practices, other forms of dress, manners, and forms of diet practiced by the people we encountered, what I witnessed and experienced on this journey in the company of my master and the other wizards who gathered has, in more ways than I even yet describe, altered what I have previously known as the boundaries and foundations of what my Master calls my reality.

So as I prepare for the next conversation between my master and my liege lord, a conversation he tells us both at its outset will be brief so that we can conclude before dark and have time to share some nourishment, I wonder how it is possible for these two beings who I serve and have come to honor so deeply manage to retain their balance in the face of the responsibilities each holds and the many simultaneous and different realms they travel to beyond the boundaries of the world the rest of us in this village in our kingdom exist within.

So, after these two noble souls greet each other, celebrate their reconnection, I have to smile when my master introduces the topic of the lesson. For it is clear that just as he so often tells me, whatever is next to be learned is always that which will always be right in front of me and which will serve me most.

Merlin's Lesson

My Son, before we begin today's lesson, I am aware that as a result that at the end our previous session on The Law of No Harm, you were left with a new understanding of both the changes that are unfolding here in your kingdom as well as some of the consequences you may face in your relationship with the King as a result of your commitment to the path of noble leadership and conscious governance.

I also know that you would have preferred that you and I have a more extensive series of conversations on the subject, following that lesson. And, indeed, you may have felt abandoned by me at that time.

Arthur nods, a little sheepishly, in agreement.

Merlin

Yes, I thought as much. But I want you to know that my choice in leaving as I did was not random; it was intentional. For the questions you were facing were and, I know, continue to be very consequential. And it would, ultimately, have been unkind and irresponsible of me to insert myself too soon in your process. These questions you face will, in all likelihood, determine the course of the rest of your life. Indeed, they will determine how you lead this kingdom and whether the legacy you leave is a continuation of the old ways or a sign of the possible changes that will eventually decide the fate of man.

I will not, at this time, enter into that dialogue with you. I do, however, believe that you will know when the time is right to do so, and at that time, you need only ask, and I will be available.

There is only one more thing I will say in the interim. I know you have been wrestling with your relationship with your father. I also know that you are disappointed in some ways in which you see him reacting and some of the decisions he is making in regard to some of the changes going on in this land. And I want to caution you to remember that he is your father. That he has consciously chosen the many things you have been exposed to, including our work together, so do not judge him harshly, or believe he is not your most ardent advocate. And certainly do not view him as your adversary,

Instead, I advise you to realize that he has arrived at the gateway to the significant change that has been evolving slowly over time. It is a change that I do not support nor do I value, but it is, based on the loss of connection to the wisdom traditions, to the honoring of natural law, and surrender to the Great Mystery. These decisions now make this change inevitable.

So, as one who stands at that gateway and feels responsible for his heritage and yours, your father will do what he can do as someone who has one foot in the old ways and one on this new and shaky ground. So acknowledge him for having the foresight to provide you with the tools and talents you will need to be a keeper of the flame of wisdom for future generations. Appreciate the tremendous challenge your father now faces, and without anger, without judgment, do all that you can to support him at this time.. But you must also recognize that there are now many courtiers who will do their best to require him to protect the only way they know, which is the one that has preserved a great disparity between those who were born to power and those who were not. So your father will have to appease those who cling to the past, especially if he is to protect your opportunity to guide this kingdom toward a more enlightened future.

So let us now take a few moments to visit the silence and allow some of these understandings to take root. Let us take some slow, deep breaths and surrender to the grace that protects us all.

Merlin, Arthur, and Aderyn sit with their eyes closed, and each, in their way, seeks solace within. Then, after a while, Merlin opens his eyes, studies
his two young charges, and when he believes they are ready, clears his throat and
begins speaking.

Merlin

As I promised on a previous occasion, let us now turn our attention to the Law of Enough. And in doing so. I invite you to consider that in ancient times, people of all tribes honored the animals that presented themselves for their nourishment, skins and furs for their warmth, the plants that gave them sustenance, healed them, and provided materials for their dwellings; the water that gave them life and the other natural elements that provided them with tools and materials to make their shelters and so much more.

In this way, there was always enough, and when, in the natural cycle of the earth, what was perceived as enough was not available, the leader and the people, always conscious of the ebb and flow of the natural law, were able to

161

turn to the Great Mystery in humility for support, solace, and make do with what was present. And they did all of this always in gratitude.

And even when there was sufficiency or abundance, each animal, resource, and natural element available to them was not only honored but used carefully and completely. Nothing was discarded or squandered. Everything had its place, its use, and was valued. Everything served a unique and distinct purpose. And when these animals, natural elements, and objects gave their lives for their well-being, their sacrifice was celebrated and acknowledged with ceremony.

You see, my Son, our ancestors studied the natural world around them and, in this way, came to know many things. They knew when it was time to move the location of their camp, they allowed themselves to be guided as to what paths to travel on, in what seasons, and which locations to visit to find the necessary foods, water, and other resources in their most plentiful supply. They understood how to read the changing seasons and determine when there might be scarcity and when there would be plenty.

This practice of being present and paying close attention to the flow and cycles of nature allowed them to stay attuned to the Law of Enough. Enough, my Son, declares itself. And those who are called leaders and are charged with the well-being of the people, understood that it was their responsibility to learn to read the signs and adapt to the changes in the Natural Flow. And, in this way, and to the best of their ability, this helped them, as much as possible, to be sure that there was enough not just for some, but for all. And when there was scarcity, what was available was shared by all and not hoarded or abused by the few.

Unfortunately, in these times, these lessons are no longer as well understood and demonstrated. Many of those who lead no longer possess the ability to even read the signs, let alone know what to do about them. They focus instead on what is directly in front of them and the pursuit of short-term goals with an eye to how it serves their advantage or that of some faction within their tribe that they favor. In this way, these so-called leaders and those they lead continue to fall more and more out of alignment with the Natural Flow.

Yes, in our time, many who lead fail to understand that an essential part of their responsibilities is not only to guide and serve those they lead, but to protect the legacy the Great Mystery places at their disposal and to ensure that those who come after them will have enough of what they will need. Many who lead today fail to recognize the interdependence of all things and thus fail to wear the mantle of true accountability for the well-being of the whole.

So study the signs, my Son. Follow the wisdom of your heart. Be sure to protect and distribute resources among all for the greater good. This, then, is the path you to follow toward noble leadership and conscious governance. And, in this way, you will stay open to the knowledge that flows to you from the Great Mystery and live by The Law of Enough.

#####

Merlin's Assignment

Spend time in contemplation and observation, and identify some of the ways man in this time has abandoned The Law of Enough. And when you have given this topic some genuine consideration, identify for yourself and those you will lead specific ways in which this condition can be corrected.

Arthur's Notes Recorded on His Parchment, Later in the Day

As my teacher was speaking on this day about the Law of Enough, I was aware that many of the laws he spoke about are obvious and true. Yet I, like many in this time, do not practice their wisdom or truly appreciate their value.

As a small boy, I remember wanting more of many things. When something sweet was presented at the end of the meal, I wanted more of it. I wanted more time when I was summoned within at the end of a day of playing in the woodlands. I wanted more time with my friends when we were engaged in games we loved, more stories when they held me in their thrall, more freedom to go further into the wilderness than I was accustomed to going when I had the opportunity. And these are just the first things that came into my mind when Merlin spoke about the Law of Enough.

So, as I consider things I have and continue to want more of, I see that my intention in most of these instances has been to have this more without regard to the impact it would have on others or even on my ability to enjoy the same thing on other occasions. As a result, I regret to say that I am no different than those among us who, as Merlin says, take more of the gifts of Natural Flow given to us by the Great Mystery than they require.

This makes me wonder how I, as a leader, can make this distinction when that hunger for more resides in me as well. How can I learn to determine where the line lies between those times when more is harmful and when it is simply part of the natural and abundant expression of life?

Notes on The Law of Enough

Study ancient times when all life forms and natural elements were honored. Everything had a place and a purpose, and nothing was discarded or abused. Study of the natural world to know how to live in true abundance and sustenance. Enough always declares itself, and the leader's responsibility is to read the signs. Enough is defined for all and not just for some. Alignment with the Natural Flow is essential for life in a physical universe.

Chapter Sixteen - The Law of Time & Timelessness

"In every deliberation, we must consider the impact
on the seventh generation
even if it requires having
skin as thick as the bark of a pine."
Great Law of the Iroquois

Aderyn's Notes

It is my liege lord Arthur who requests the time for the next conversation. And it is clear to me that this timing appears to be sooner than my master expects. It is also clear that Merlin is engaged in something he considers important, something that he will have to interrupt to meet with young Arthur. And yet, as is often the case in many things, Merlin demonstrates the truth of his teachings. He smiles and tells me to accept young Arthur's request.

He then pauses a moment and, in answer to my unvoiced question, explains that if he is to be true to the practice of the laws he is in the process of sharing with Arthur, he must be attuned to the point in time when his student begins to become one with the lessons. He must then do his best to encourage his students' enthusiasm and commitment, even if it is inconvenient or interrupts some other activity.

So, as I prepare the cottage for the conversation and then go in search of my liege lord, who is delighted and honored that Merlin has accepted his request so quickly, I am once again reminded of the tremendous privilege being afforded to me to be in service to Merlin and to be a party to these lessons.

When my Liege Lord arrives and he joins Merlin and me on the slight rise beside the cottage where I have set up our chairs, this understanding is reinforced by the way Merlin greets Arthur.

He first acknowledges that he is clear that Arthur has something he wishes to talk about and that he has taken the initiative in asking that they meet. He then asks him if it is something of an immediate nature or if it can wait until after exploring this day's topic, which might have some bearing on what it is that Arthur wants to talk about

When I hear Merlin say this, I have to smile, as does Arthur, for we both have experienced countless moments with Merlin when he appears to have far more knowledge about what is in our minds before we even speak of it.

When Arthur assents to Merlin and reports that his topic can be addressed after the session, Merlin tells my liege lord that if he has time, we can also share some nourishment and then talk at leisure.

Again, I find myself smiling at the courtesy and honor of Merlin as the teacher is showing his student. Then Merlin invites us into the silence, allowing a little longer than usual, and then begins speaking.

Merlin's Lesson

My Son, let us speak today about the mysteries of time and timelessness. And let us begin by remembering that what has already occurred will never recur in quite the same way again. And what has yet to occur can be considered, anticipated, and even envisioned, but cannot yet be fully experienced. Only that which is directly before us in the present moment offers us the opportunity to participate fully, discover its scope and import, learn the level of skill required, and demonstrate the mastery that can result.

As a whole, the children of man and, most specifically, many of those who aspire to lead or who already occupy positions of leadership in these troubled times, appear to have forgotten much of the wisdom suggested by this law. Instead, they often remain confined within the illusion of time and either place the majority of their attention on the past and search there for some ground to understand, or some theory or rationale to justify some action in the present, or they allow what they fear or hope will occur in the future to color their experience in the present. In this way, they miss the opportunity to fully experience the gold of opportunity that is right before them; the opportunity to express their gratitude to the Great Mystery for the experience, to be open to discoveries, new learnings, and much more in the present moment.

In the case of leaders who remain captive to the past, there is what can best be called a double jeopardy. For they not only do they limit their inexperience, but they also put at risk that of those they serve. And do not underestimate the number of leaders who fall into this category, and whose natural response is to struggle mightily and futilely in their effort to stop time and to try to continually recreate the familiar. But of course, as the Law of Time and Timelessness tells us, what has passed cannot be recreated, and what has yet to be cannot yet be fully engaged in.

I say this because by believing either of these experiences is possible, these leaders weigh themselves down as well as those they lead by dwelling not on finding solutions to whatever obstacles or opportunities are arising in the present, but also fail to prepare to address those that may arise in the future. Instead, they focus on what they or others appear to have done in the past that, most likely, is no longer relevant and cannot be changed or altered..

As a result, this type of leader often finds himself in a landscape of frustration, troubled by the debilitating distempers, doubts, and regrets. And too often these energies also mask a deeper experience, which is fear – fear of the unknown, fear of that which is the new, fear of a possible loss of power if they do not respond to the moment adequately, and, ultimately, fear of not knowing which, as you may have felt or noticed in others, is almost greater than their fear of their physical death which they and many other mistakenly believe to be the end of all things.

These leaders, trapped in the past, express disdain and enmity towards those who advance the cause of moment-to-moment awareness and optimism for the possibilities that lie ahead. These leaders also suffer from a distortion of vision that impedes their ability to see what is truly remarkable right in front of them, and to participate in wonder and awe for all that has not yet come into being.

As awkward and ineffective as these states of mind and emotions may be, many who wear this human form and rise to or lay claim to positions of leadership cling to these habituated practices with a tenacity that defies logic and reason, and obscures both clarity and the gift of imagination allows and the joy of dealing with the moment with curiosity and the spirit of play.

Indeed, this all-too-traditional and habituated response by many leaders is like watching one walking backwards, carrying some ungainly and heavy burdens, and insisting that those who follow them do the same while proclaiming their intention of reaching the next destination quickly and easily.

Merlin pauses here and asks Aderyn to share any experience he may have have had while he and Merlin were on their last journey that might speak to this tendency.

Aderyn

What comes to mind, Master, is the time when you were invited to speak on one of the most remarkable healings that a number of the wizards in the conclave had ever witnessed. And yet, you kept being interrupted by that Wizard from the Southern Kingdom, who was envious of both your skill and your reputation.

Merlin

And what did you make of his efforts?

Aderyn

They were futile. I can remember the looks exchanged between the other wizards. But he was so focused on trying to gain their attention that he was not present enough to appreciate that he was losing it.

Merlin

Aderyn...Arthur, in ways, the same observation can be made for those who call themselves leaders and who spend the majority of their time and energy focused exclusively on themselves and what is called the future. While some suggest this is a sign of a leader's vision and celebrate him for having foresight, as one who aspires to be a noble leader, I encourage you to first determine if the attention you focus in this way is part of your dialogue with the Great Mystery or is this focus a diversion and avoidance, prompted by your desire, and the illusion that what lies ahead will somehow magically be better than what is currently occurring,, even and especially, when you are not doing what needs to be done in the present to create such a future.

Being aware of these habituated patterns of response to either the past or the future, and focusing as much as possible on the present moment, where challenges and opportunities can be addressed. As will be your ability to separate wishful thinking from reality and fantasy from imagination, true vision and commitment to the greater good, from illusions and false assumptions. Yes, if you want to create a future that is better than or, at the very least, equal to the present, you must remain focused in the present, for that is where all action occurs.

These differences require practical understanding, perseverance, and a patient and enduring commitment to do the courageous work of turning concepts and images produced by the imagination into tangible realities.

So, do your best to effectively observe and identify the challenges and opportunities that may arise. Acknowledge that there may be lessons learned in the past that can apply in the present. And also stay open to what is new and not previously encountered. Always demonstrate the courage and wit to consult both inner and external sources of guidance and have the patience to await clear and cogent answers before proceeding. And, in this way, these practices and ingredients will support you and those you lead to chart a course as effective and achievable as possible in each present moment, knowing that what you and they do in each present moment will shape the future.

Yes, if you aspire to lead with nobility and consciousness, also do your best to envision the future as a clean canvas on which you can inscribe in great detail more constructive and ideal outcomes that will uplift and celebrate your virtues and talents, and those contributed by those you lead. This type of envisioning is always best accomplished when you step out of time and merge with the Great Mystery in that which is called timelessness, which I will say more about shortly.

It will be of value to you to also remember that each present moment also includes both physical and psychological or emotional time. So sufficient understanding of both and the ability to differentiate between them will open a much greater understanding of the Natural Flow and the Great Mystery. The present moment, then, is always the doorway to genuine opportunity! And if you find that you are uncomfortable in the present moment, you would be wise to investigate why that is the case. Or you will be continually dragging your discomfort into It is the canvas on which you can paint a legacy of true nobility, consciousness, and genuine love and compassion for those you lead.

So measure when, where, and how to engage in physical and psychological time. When to use present moment awareness to evaluate the fruits of the past and execute the necessary decisions that will guide the present and impact the future.

This council is not intended to deter or discourage you from also experiencing timelessness. Timelessness, or what some call the space between moments, will allow you to let your vision take full flight. It is the dimension in which you can exercise the full scope of your imagination and follow your intuition. It is the place in which prayer, reflection, and true communion with the Great Mystery can occur without concern for the ordinary tasks that occupy you and demand your attention in the dimension of time. Indeed, timelessness is the realm in which you can soar without the constraints encountered in physical and psychological time.

Timelessness is the realm unfettered and unlimited by attachment to a result. It is a dimension in which you need not be limited by questions of rewards, goals, or temporal measures of success. Timelessness is the realm in which you can connect with your true genius and the full measure of your heart without limitation. Timelessness is the counterbalance, the gift that is available to you that allows you to celebrate and, as a result, to experience life from a different perspective.

So, My Son, I encourage you to accept this gift, be grateful for it, and always use it wisely. From timelessness, you will bring back the fruits of your explorations to this dimension of time and space, and I invite you to encourage those you lead to do the same so that everyone can manifest the gifts they receive during their explorations and invest them in time and space for the greater good.

If you remember that on this physical, earthly plane and within this conceit that is called time and space, energy follows or is shaped by thought into manifestation. This understanding will motivate you to enter the realm of timelessness and recognize that thought is not the beginning, but instead issues from both the subtle and greater aspects of unfettered imagination.

For this reason, I encourage you to explore and experiment with this Law of Time and Timelessness. You will discover that it will, indeed, be a valuable ally to you as you progress on this path to nobility and consciousness.

#####

Merlin's Assignment

Consider how you counter what appear to be the natural tendencies that haunt all who wear this human form to give purchase to doubt, impatience, and the sadness and regret that cause you to fall out of alignment with the natural flow and the greater good.

Then identify how you know when it is appropriate to remain in time and when it is appropriate to surrender to timelessness.

Lastly, consider how you counter what appear to be the natural tendencies that haunt all who wear this human form to give purchase to doubt, impatience, sadness, and regret. For it is these emotions that generally cause one to fall out of alignment with the natural flow and the greater good.

Arthur's Notes Recorded on His Parchment, Later in the Day

I am still always amazed that Merlin can understand what it is that I intend to say before I say it and find the most unexpected ways to address it. This was the case today when I went to talk to him about the trouble I am having making the wealth of information he is sharing with me. At times, I feel an enormous obligation to honor the gifts he gives me and an equal sense of responsibility to be certain that I will use them to the benefit of the people I will one day lead.

And then, before I shared any of this with him, he spoke of the difference between time and timelessness and in those moments not only addressed my unasked questions but helped me to change my view of things, and reminded me of a time in my life when I understood that some actions and events in my world fit more naturally into time and space, while others clearly belonged in timelessness and this was long before I was aware of the meaning of these two terms.

As a small child, I understood that the dimensions of time and timelessness were both real and equally important. Although I must admit that I loved being in timelessness more than being in time.

But as I have grown older, I somehow lost this understanding and, as a result, my life has become more difficult. And I cannot say exactly when this happened. Only that when it did, it brought conflict and frustration into my life. For when I lost the ability to distinguish between these two dimensions, I tried to do things that are best done within time in timelessness, and, of even greater challenge, I tried to do things in time that are only possible in timelessness.

So in just a few moments today, Merlin gave me back the means to organize my life and do all that I can do in their appropriate dimensions. And already I can sense that this understanding will reduce my frustration and greatly increase my joy.

Notes on Time and Timelessness

Avoid being trapped in either the past or the future – the first is unrepeatable, and the second has yet to occur. Focus on every present moment to learn, to understand, and to chart a necessary course on the immediate path. Allow present-moment awareness and a true understanding of physical and psychological time to give one entry into the Great Mystery. Celebrate the full use of imagination and fascination in the space beyond time called timelessness. Return from visits to the zone of timelessness with the fruits of one's visit. The Law of Time and Timelessness is an invaluable ally.

Chapter Seventeen - The Law of Harmony, Joy, Beauty & Light

"Beauty is eternity gazing at itself in a mirror."
Khalil Gibran

Aderyn's Notes

As I arrange the chairs on the rise beside the cottage, place the cups containing Merlin's favorite morning brew of herbs that I prepared for my master and my liege lord earlier, and arrange my place from which I can best hear and most easily transcribe the contents of their next conversation without intruding upon them, I find myself called to pause and take in the remarkable beauty that is unfolding in the natural world around me.

The early morning light seems, at this moment, so pure and fresh. It softly illuminates some sections of the ground, touches some of the leaves softly, and leaves others still in the shadows. It also highlights the abundant clusters of wildflowers that rise from the fragrant grasses that will soon be tall and will dance in the winds. The sunlight also touches the canopies of leaves near the tops of the trees. And this display of beauty is complemented by the birds whose sounds are varied and sweet, and by a rich scent rising from the earth, still slightly moist from an early morning shower. This remarkable vista calls out to my heart and awakens in me a sense of deep gratitude for the many gifts the Great Mystery presents to all, without exception, who are willing to pause and grant it witness.

As my master exits the cottage and joins me, he smiles warmly and for a moment stands beside me, his hand resting gently on my shoulder. While I am often clear that he holds me in good regard, I sense, in that place beyond words, that this is a special moment of intimacy between us. I also sense that he, with his silence, is encouraging me to go deeper into this union with the natural world.

It is at this moment that young Arthur arrives. He and my master share their usual warm and enthusiastic greeting. Then my liege lord turns to me, greets me as well, and with a generosity of spirit, he thanks me for capturing the content of his sessions with Merlin, which he knows will be a valuable aid to him not only in the days ahead, but for years to come when he will be in service as the King. While Arthur is often generous in his praise of others, it seems, in this moment, that the Great Mystery has indeed conspired to make this morning even more special. And when my master begins speaking, I find myself smiling at the perfect coincidence between his topic and the wonders of this day.

Merlin's Lesson

My Son, let us speak this morning about this opportunity that is yours within every moment of your life. The opportunity to seek, above all else, that which is light, filled with joy, harmony, and of great consequence and beauty.

This advice issues from my heart and from the understanding that most challenges you will encounter in life will result when you allow yourself to be seduced and, in this way, blinded by any one of the many illusions that arise if you turn away from the Natural Flow. Indeed, most of the pain and suffering, and most certainly, the tendency to miss the true gifts offered by the Great Mystery, occur on this physical plane when one becomes attached to expectations regarding specific outcomes in pursuit of goals that issue from our minds and when we are bound too exclusively by the laws of reason and of physical time, space and form.

This attachment to expectations and specific outcomes places an impossible demand on the Great Mystery, which is itself limitless and timeless, whole and unifying. It asks the Great Mystery, which in its entirety is unknowable and infinite, to disclose itself to us only in ways that are known to us and that are, therefore, limited.

It is, of course, an absurd and contradictory expectation, especially when one stops to consider that this request causes one to miss what is most precious and true. What is most unique, mysterious, harmonious, and beautiful in each person, event, and moment? This attachment and expectation that the Great Mystery will conform to our limited beliefs and expectations also prevents us from experiencing the gifts of spontaneity, fascination, and originality – all of which are among the most precious gifts the Great Mystery offers us.

So remember that these and other habituated practices and attachments can cause you and those you serve to remain ensnared in the illusion of separation rather than the experience of unity and wholeness. They also cause us to believe that resistance rather than trust and surrender is the path we should follow, that competition rather than cooperation is natural, and that illusion and fear, rather than truth and light, are natural conditions.

Merlin pauses here and invites both Arthur and Aderyn to take a few moments
and go within to a place, a favorite place that calls out a sense of wonder and awe
in them. And so for a few quiet moments, Merlin enjoys studying the faces of these
young men as they take their inner journeys.

After a while, and before Arthur and Aderyn fully return their attention to the

present moment, Merlin begins to speak in almost a whisper.

My young companions, before you open your eyes, mark this moment and what you have done to arrive here. This space of quiet and silence, of beauty, harmony, and light is always yours to visit, to renew, refresh, and to remember. This is a gift of grace that you can always use to avoid being held captive by some of the illusions and delusions that periodically visit all of us who wear this human form.

Yes, remember that no matter how strong your experience of the darkness may be, no matter how long you may find yourself in it, it is an essential component of the natural Flow and is always followed by the return of the light, and therefore by an experience of rebirth and innocence.

And this aspect of the Law of Harmony, Joy, Beauty, and Light is demonstrated in so many ways in the physical world, if you will but use your eyes not just to look but to see, your ears not just to listen but to hear, and your heart not just to feel, but to open to the miracles happening in each moment.

Now open your eyes and see this miracle unfolding around us. Mark the fact that the rising of the sun comes after the hours of darkness; that darkness of an interior space disappears the moment you walk out into the light; that limiting impact of a dark mood caused by too exclusive a focus on negative emotions such as fear, worry, doubt, and confusion, is lightened almost immediately if you look with the innocent eyes of the child that always lives within you at what is unfolding around you. Yes, all you need do is to focus on your next breath, on the sound of laughter, the warmth of the sun, the scent of a flower, the sound of individual drops of rain falling upon a dry patch of earth, on the relief brought by a fresh gust of wind, the almost infinite symphony of sound issuing from the winged ones who soar at dawn. Yes, these gifts of grace, in an almost infinite number, are yours and belong to all whom you will ever lead.

This is why I remind you of the wisdom contained in the Law of Time and Timelessness and now, on this day, in the Law of Harmony, Joy, Beauty, and Light. So befriend these laws and allow them to remind you and those you serve that just as we sometimes become captured by the limitations of physical and psychological time, we also sometimes become captured by the darkness that is a part of the duality that exists here on the physical plane.

So be transparent with those you serve and share your vulnerability as well as your experiences with the illusions that periodically capture all of us. Do so with genuine honesty and transparency, and you will assist those you serve to better and more quickly regain their balance and reconnect to the light when they become captured by the darkness.

Also, help them to remember that darkness is a natural phenomenon that provides those of us who reside here on the planet with the opportunity to learn how to break free from the boundaries of time, space, and form. Remind them that one of your tasks as a leader is to help them understand and move beyond the experiences of separation, resistance, fear, and isolation that arise periodically within us all, and in this way, you will encourage those you lead to do the same.

Remind them that false assumptions and untested beliefs are dispelled not through arcane practices, not through the application of leeches or the mutilation of the flesh, not by total abstinence and other forms of unnatural denial of life's true wonders, but simply and always by opening to the wisdom of Natural Flow. Remind them to look up and out when they become captured by emotions and illusions that sometimes cause them to look down and away; to look wide rather than only close at hand, and in this way to see, once again, the true harmony, beauty, and lightness of life.

Yes, your companions, turn your attention and encourage those you serve to also turn theirs to the present moment. Encourage them to hold close the knowledge that in every being, every object, and every event, there is something magnificent and wondrous, something that is part of the design of the Great Mystery. Do this, and you and those you lead, those you heal, will truly walk on the path of nobility and greater consciousness.

Indeed, you will be wise to consider this to be one of your most important tasks – to celebrate and encourage this understanding and awareness in yourself and in those you serve. Remind yourself and others that life is a gift, even those times and aspects that appear as great challenges and seemingly insurmountable obstacles. Remember that even when people, events, and experiences arise that appear designed to keep you and those you serve confined in limitation, a small shift of focus away from this illusion, and its possible negative consequences, a small shift away from negative emotions and toward the light will often prove to be all that is required to allow the light to illuminate the darkness and the joy, harmony and beauty to once again take their rightful place in your consciousness.

Remember as well that engaging in the many forms of creative expression that are natural to man - art, music, dance, storytelling in word and movement, the practice of crafts that put one in touch with the natural fibers, the colors, scents, and textures of the earth, are invaluable. As are all of the activities that involve sharing kindness, compassion, and wisdom with others. These creative expressions that encourage the development of new skills, methods, and systems that can advance daily existence, as well as the nurturing care of children, the exploration of the natural world, experimentation with new ways to maximize the use of resources, better care of the sources of our food, water and air that are the sources of our nourishment, play, celebration and always the ability to go more deeply into the silence and commune with the wisdom that offers deep renewal, and finally surrender to the Great Mystery. These are all keys present in the practice of The Lay of Beauty, Joy, Harmony, and Light.

Encourage and demonstrate this truth, and you will, in turn, contribute to the greater well-being and happiness of all who are a part of this or any other realm you ever inhabit. Indeed, in this way, as your well-being becomes more pervasive, so will that of those you lead.

Yes, practice this law, and it will contribute to your love and honoring of life.

#####

Merlin's Assignment

There are natural paths that you, as a leader, can follow in supporting those you serve to invite and encourage them to move beyond the imprisonment of illusions and to experience and celebrate harmony, beauty, joy, and light. So, take some time to identify as many of these paths as you can, and also identify a few examples of how these paths can be better demonstrated in your daily life.

Arthur's Notes Recorded on His Parchment, Later in the Day

How blessed I feel this day. As words in the lesson on The Law of Harmony, Joy, Beauty, and Light passed through my teacher to Aderyn and me, I felt a sense of excitement grow within me.

To have this opportunity to serve my people and to have as one of my goals offering encouragement and invitation to them to celebrate the precious gifts of the Great Mystery is such an honor and privilege. To be in the position to remind them to inherit more of the gifts they have come here to share. To have this opportunity to remind myself and others of the joy of learning and of immersing ourselves in fascination, and in the search for originality and meaning, what more could I or anyone ever ask?

Only, I guess, that I will have the requisite courage, compassion and under-standing, perseverance and commitment, and, of course, the skill to fulfill my role in this sacred relationship. It is an awareness that fills my heart with joy, but also gives me pause. For this is no small responsibility.

Notes on The Law of Harmony, Joy, Beauty, and Light

Seek above all else that which is light and filled with joy, harmony, and beauty. Darkness that occurs as part of the natural flow is always followed by new light. Most pain and suffering come from attachment to an outcome and from the departure from the gifts present in each moment. Illusions, limiting beliefs, fear, worry, and doubt lead to unnatural states. The noble leader deals first with these forms of darkness within himself so he can best deal with them in the external world. Lightness, joy, harmony, beauty, and, above all, a genuine love of life are the gifts a leader can bestow on those he serves.

Chapter Eighteen - The Law of Transformation

"When we quit thinking primarily about ourselves
and our self-preservation,
We undergo a truly heroic transformation
of consciousness."
–Joseph Campbell

Adreyn's Note

My master and I have not spoken in days. Although I have prepared his meals and gone about my daily tasks in service to him, he has spent his time out of sight in that special part of the cottage that is reserved solely for tasks that are still beyond the scope of my capacity and understanding. I have, however, periodically been given access to this room in order to clean this private space, and on occasion, to receive instruction in one of the lesser healing arts that he has begun to give me instruction in.

When he has not been occupied in this way, he has occasionally appeared, visible in body, but his mind and focus have been elsewhere, and then, without a word as to his destination or time of return, he has gone off alone into the forest.

At such times, I know that my task is not to disturb him and to wait patiently in attendance, ready to provide him, as best as I can, with whatever he requires.

Finally, after days of this behavior, he returned early this afternoon from one of these visits to the forest and asked that I find my liege lord and invite him to come to the cottage for the next conversation.

When I find young Arthur, it appears that he, like me, has been patiently awaiting word, knowing that when his teacher becomes otherwise engaged, there is little he can do but wait.

Returning to the cottage, accompanied by my liege lord, Merlin does not stand on ceremony, nor does he refer, in any way, to the tasks that have occupied him. Instead, he invites us both into the silence and then, after a while, begins speaking in a low and soft voice that appears to be trying to find ease of expression, after a time when it has not been used.

Merlin's Lesson

It is time we explore another essential aspect of your responsibility, Arthur, as a leader, and yours, Aderyn, as a healer. This is a responsibility you have both to yourself and to those you serve, and it is to leave each person, event, object, and experience you encounter at least as well or better off than when you first encounter them or it. This is one of the highest forms of spiritual alchemy that you can perform. And this is the territory of the Law of Transformation.

So always seek to transform the dross of the seemingly ordinary into the gold of higher value and expanded consciousness. Always take the mundane and the habitual and seek to uncover within these seemingly ordinary events, experiences, and encounters that which is unique and special. Always seek to convert the discarded to a higher and better use, and to take the boundary of the known and the familiar and expand and stretch it further toward the miraculous. In short, always invest curiosity, imagination, and fascination in exploring the precious gift of existence that has been given to you by the Great Mystery.

Yes, turning the dross of everyday experience, habituated behaviors, and limiting beliefs into the gold of knowledge and wisdom is not just the key to a life of genuine value and meaning; it is, indeed, the very reason that the spirit breathes through you.

Following this path, however, I remind you, is no easy task. But with courage and perseverance, you will assist yourself and others to turn each moment from one of struggle and confusion into one of engagement, learning, and immeasurable value.

Deny that this is the purpose of life; pretend that life is about repeating the same practices and concepts over and over again, and that leadership and healing are about utilizing these practices and concepts to gain and maintain power over others, and you will miss the mark. Focus on accumulating more wealth than you require to sustain your existence, inflate your role in service to your self-image, or attempt to fill wounds that cannot and will never be filled through any of these practices or experiences, and you will rapidly find yourself out of alignment with the Great Mystery. And this, too often in our time, is precisely the offense committed by those who call themselves leaders.

This is equally true of efforts to accumulate and try to control nature's resources, not for the preservation of these resources or the greater good of the greatest number, but instead to bring benefit to oneself or only to a specific segment of the people in this kingdom or any other. To do any of these things will violate natural law.

So if you are desirous of demonstrating noble leadership and the mastery of the healing arts, always remember that nature's resources are an extension of the Great Mystery and the property of all. To treat them otherwise is to distort your sacred task.

These and other foundational understandings are essential if you seek to lead with nobility. And to lead for any other purpose is, as we have discussed many times, not to lead at all, but simply to visit upon the people one is responsible for the illusion of separation, of superiority, and the sins of fear, ignorance, and scarcity, all of which are distortions of truth.

So, if you aspire to serve, know that advancing any limited beliefs or restrictive practices constitutes an abdication of integrity. Such behaviors and practices also betray the knowledge writ large in the pages of humanity's record, that it is not the destination but the journey. Not the result but the process and all of the fruits of experience and wisdom that issue from it, which are among life's most precious gifts.

Merlin pauses and smiles.

Quite a dance, isn't it? Arthur, my son. Take a moment to share a way that you can focus your attention on elevating the process and celebrating life in this way in each moment.

Arthur

I must admit, my teacher, that there are moments when your gift of being able to translate the art of leadership and healing into words is both remarkable and very intimidating. So as I sit here, wanting nothing more than to answer your question and please you, T find myself at a loss. Forgive me.

Merlin

Your humility and honesty, Arthur, are worthy answers to my request. And you need never apologize for either. I also hope that one day, you will come to accept that both traits are the foundation of true wisdom and ultimately, steps on the path toward enlightenment.

Yes, if you remain faithful to these gifts, I assure you, you will do your part admirably in exposing the inherent flaws in the limited beliefs that have haunted humanity from the earliest times, beliefs that posit that scarcity rather than abundance, deprivation rather than sharing, aggression and conquest rather than alignment and cooperation, obedience, and surrender to the wisdom of heart are all essential conditions for the elevation of consciousness.

So, My Son, never apologize for humility and honesty. Would that all who walk this earth be so blessed.

Also remember, Arthur, that your responsibility as a noble and conscious leader, and yours, Aderyn, as a healer and practitioner of the healing arts, will be to replace the lie that these limiting conditions are the goal of the Great Mystery. No, these and other distortions result from too exclusive a dependence by man on reason, too obsessive an adherence to the false laws of self-interest, and too rigid a confinement within physical time, space, and form.

Also, remember these distortions always arise when the leader and healer lose their way and those they serve cease to study the Natural Flow, and forget that any one cycle will not be permanent but only a temporary condition experienced on the path leading to the next cycle and to the next destination, which can be as wondrous as you and those you serve can allow.

This is not to say that you should not observe yourself and those you lead, and acknowledge when you or they become captured by one of these limiting beliefs. But be not harsh in your judgment, but instead be vigilant and mindful and remind yourself and those you serve that life is a learning ground, and that these and other false starts, flawed methods, and distortions of truth are valuable lessons that must be encountered on the path of evolving consciousness.

Nor is this to say that in acknowledging this understanding, you should permit yourself or others to continue to impede or obstruct positive and constructive ways of living. Instead, let these experiences serve as reminders that it is part of your responsibility as a leader and that of those you lead to educate, invite, encourage, support, and inform yourself and others who wander off the path to turn once again toward the greater good.

And in instances where this instructive and encouraging approach is not sufficient, as a leader and a healer you are counseled to use true insight and the gift of enlightened governance to set temporary boundaries and establish laws that limit the power of any individual to impose detrimental control over others, to bring injury to other life forms and harm to this precious environment on which all life depends for its survival.

Indeed, just as you would place stakes in the ground to protect the fragile sapling from damage by wind, you are encouraged to provide the temporary means to guide and protect those who you serve and who suffer from distortions of beliefs and unnatural practices from injuring themselves and others until their consciousness is sufficiently elevated to ensure that they will act responsibly and in accord with the greater good.

In all instances and to the best of your ability, avoid the use of the lesser and negative tools we have discussed, such as the manipulation of truth, the threat of punishment, and loss of individual freedoms that, in many ways, cause the distortions of beliefs and unnatural practices in the first place. These imperfect practices, utilized by some who call themselves leaders and healers, do not support the expansion of human consciousness but continue the illusion that the children of man cannot be trusted and that resident goodness is not the natural inclination of all.

So, young companions, I encourage you to practice the Law of Transformation and demonstrate compassion for the individual, and an even greater compassion for the whole. Demonstrate courage and act as a champion of truth. Demonstrate your role as a servant of the Great Mystery and demonstrate compassion, forgiveness, and understanding of those you lead. In this way, you will empower yourself and those you lead to find the way out of the prison of ignorance and into a greater experience of the majesty and oneness that is the true and Great Mystery.

#####

Merlin's Assignment

Seek to identify some of the many ways that you can turn the dross of the ordinary and the habitual into the gold of the unique and the special.

Arthur's Notes Recorded on His Parchment, Later in the Day

On this day, my teacher gave me a deeper understanding of my role. One of the true challenges I face, he said, in becoming a noble and conscious leader, and in the case of Aderyn becoming a true healer is our willingness to follow the path that leads ourselves and others to a higher destination and, of even greater consequence, to maintain our purchase on this path and continue moving in the right direction when either of us or those we serve step off it.

It sounds so clear, true, and simple when he speaks, and I know that what Merlin says on this subject is true. And yet I also know that these things are easier to talk about, but often difficult to accomplish.

So, in this moment, fresh from being in that special energy and spirit that surrounds my teacher during these sessions, I know that, whether difficult or not, I must be diligent in the practice of this Law of Transformation. I must do my best to measure each of my interactions with the people of this realm, with the four-legged, winged, and finned creatures and with what my teacher calls the essential elements as well – the sky, the earth, the water, the wind and the fire spirits that I encounter, and in this way, measure all of this by my ability and willingness to leave them better or, at the very least, at the level they are at when I first encounter them. If I can do this, I trust that my time as a leader will be of genuine value to those I serve.

Notes on The Law of Transformation

Always leave each person, event, and action one encounters better than one has found it. Always turn the dross of the ordinary and the habitual into the gold of the unique and the special. This law is not just a key to a life of greater meaning and value; it is the underlying purpose of life. Attempting to control nature's resources or the children of man for personal gain is contrary to natural law. It is the role of the noble leader to provide sufficient structure and governance to support higher consciousness. It is the role of the noble leader to demonstrate compassion for the individual and, therefore, celebrate the whole.

Chapter Nineteen - The Law of Dreaming

"Each man should frame life so that at some
future hour fact and his dreaming meet."
-Victor Hugo

Aderyn's Notes

My liege lord Arthur arrives at midday as arranged. His cloak and boots are wet from the heavy rain that has been falling all morning. As I open the door for him and he enters, however, I notice that on the horizon, there is a break in the dark clouds. When he sees me look in that direction, he invites me to look further to the East, where I can see a broad and vibrant multi-colored rainbow arcing its way across the distant sky.

Although it is not his custom to share many details with me about his life beyond this cottage where we meet, the fact that we have both been engaged in this series of sessions with my master has deepened our connection, and for this, I am most grateful. My liege lord is truly a remarkable young man, and I am certain that I will have the privilege of witnessing him accomplish many things of genuine value during his reign.

As he is in the process of taking off his cloak and boots, and we await Merlin's appearance, however, he thanks me for the service I am performing in transcribing the lessons. He then asks if he might come, from time to time, when my master is away or otherwise engaged, to read copies of earlier sessions and perhaps ask my opinion about some of the notes he has been taking. Writing is not, he says, one of his most developed skills, and it is important to him that he captures the essence of Merlin's communications.

His comment surprises me, and I tell him this. I also assure him that the notes from the previous lessons that he has asked me to hold, along with the notes I have transcribed, contradict his assessment of his skill level.

He thanks me but goes on to say that he understands that there is much more he can learn and asks if I will assist him in this. I take this as another sign and confirmation of his uniqueness as a being and his commitment to prepare for his future responsibilities with integrity. It also confirms the evolution of his leadership skills, for as our future king, he could easily have ordered me to perform this task, but instead, by nature and as a result of the guidance he has received over the years from my master, he invites my participation.

I am still considering this fact when Merlin enters and calls us into stillness in preparation for the next lesson.

Merlin's Lesson

My Son, let us talk today about the fact that many refer to that which they experience in their daily lives as '*reality*' and that which they sometimes remember from the hours when they slumber as '*dreaming.*'

However, having been schooled in inquiry and self-discovery, and having become more practiced in the exploration of both inner and outer dimensions, you now know that this distinction is arbitrary and contributes to the various illusions, misconceptions, and false distinctions that allow the majority of us who occupy this human form to divide our consciousness. This false distinction also perpetuates misunderstandings regarding the true nature of the Great Mystery.

Indeed, those less informed, and unfortunately, I include among them a number who, in this time, call themselves leaders, have not yet discovered that the willingness to explore the boundaries of human consciousness and pass through the fires of direct experience that will burn away ignorance and fear. Instead, they cling to what they call reality, and in the process, disregard or diminish the extraordinary value of dreaming.

These individuals are generally those who give exclusive sovereignty to what are called facts and reason. They also focus exclusively on what their physical senses record in their interaction with the external world. As a result, they are cynical about that which cannot be immediately validated or translated by these tools. This is, of course, understandable, but it is also regrettable.

For as you are beginning to learn, there are extraordinary realms that lie beyond the reach of reason. To experience them, however, one must be willing to surrender the illusion that we who wear this human form have control over existence. One must also surrender the belief that the boundaries of time, physical space and form, and facts and reason are the only elements that exist on his physical plane.

In short, there are some individuals – and unfortunately, in these troubled times, their number is large – who remain trapped within these boundaries of time, space, and form and worship only fact and reason. And, as a result, they fail to experience for themselves and, in the process, discourage others from exploring the true gifts, joy, and wonder that await each of us when we acknowledge the values of timelessness and dreaming.

Of course, these illusions that occupy the majority of the members of the human herd are not purely negative. Time, physical form, and space, fact, and reason play their part in the duality that is found on this physical plane. And this duality provides us with the opportunity to learn some important lessons, gain experience in the rules that govern time and space, but it does not allow us to discover the freedom of timelessness and the true joy and magic of surrendering to dreaming.

Therefore, the most important task you, as a conscious leader, can undertake is to contribute, at least whenever possible, to encouraging those you serve to first be aware that there are these other planes that exist beyond the boundaries of the five senses. Speak to some of the hints and clues that exist in their daily realities that point to what lies beyond reality. The flashes of intuition or insight about events or encounters with others that precede a physical encounter. The sense of familiarity one has in an encounter, although there are no so-called facts to support it. The sense that someone is about to say a thing and then to have that someone speak it.

These are just hints and clues that there is more to life than, as we so often say, meets the eye. You can also introduce others to the concept of timelessness and dreaming by speaking the truth, and always from your heart, about your personal experience. And you can also share some of the challenges you encounter and some of the gifts you have received in your journeys in these other dimensions. In this way, you will shed light on the value of these alternatives and encourage those you serve to understand that they need not treat life as an impenetrable prison called reality.

Also, let them know that what prevents them from exploring timelessness and dreaming is not other beings, the scarcity of resources, the absence of wealth or power, but many of the illusions and false beliefs that have been put in place by past generations of man that they mistakenly accept, practice, and propagate.

So remind those you serve that trust and surrender, a willingness to exper-iment, to observe the play of children, and remember some of their own experiences when they passed through those periods of their lives, when imaginary friends others could not see were more valuable than the things their parents and teachers insisted were more important. Encourage them to spend more time daydreaming so they can begin to re-experience the freedom and wonder that is always available to them when they practice the Law of Dreaming. Yes, remind them that all they need to do is to turn away, even if only occasionally, from their quest for a tangible result and reward, and approach the practice of this law with curiosity and fascination.

Also, introduce them to the art of breathing and following their breath more deeply into the silence.. Introduce them to experiencing that place when they no longer have to work to breathe, but can experience themselves being breathed. Encourage them to practice the art of seeing by adjusting the angle of their heads, as I have shown you, and narrowing their eyes to experience the other planes that exist beneath and beside the normal canvas of the world. For some, you can encourage the use of some of the magic plants and herbs that provide access to these parallel realms that exist within and beyond the physical realm, a discovery that will forever alter their understanding of the Great Mystery, and allow them to experience what is new and fresh, authentic, and filled with joy and wonder.

My son, your willingness to become an instrument for the exploration of these truths will allow those you lead to ease aside the veil so that they can experience that reality is only one of the temporary conditions through which humanity learns some of life's essential lessons. And in this way, they will come to appreciate the time spent in these other dimensions and also become aware that anytime they choose, they can pierce the veil and discover the precious gift of dreaming and the gifts that other dimensions can provide them. And perhaps, the most valuable of these gifts will be the understanding that they do not have to become so concerned by the events and experiences of temporal life, nor do they need to hold onto their fears of death and what lies beyond this plane.

#####

Merlin's Assignment

Just as you have learned to discover the pause between the in-breath and the out-breath and how this pause gives you entrance into a deeper aspect of the Great Mystery, seek now to spend more time in the place where your dreaming and what most call reality meet, and where this portal can lead you and those you serve.

Arthur's Notes Recorded on His Parchment, Later in the Day

This day, as my teacher spoke about the Law of Dreaming, I began to remember that early in my years under his protection and guidance, he introduced me to what he called "the unseen world." Of course, in the beginning, I rarely experienced what he described. And for a time, I wondered if I was deficient in some way and would never be able to see in the way he encouraged. But after a time and with greater practice, I was able to follow his guidance, relax more, and allow rather than attempt to make seeing happen.

He taught me how to hold my head in a particular way to see things that otherwise remained invisible. He taught me how to enter the pause between my breaths. He taught me how to listen between the normal physical sounds that I was accustomed to hearing. And finally, he taught me that when I stop straining and trying too hard, what I was attempting to see, hear, feel, and comprehend was often right there in front of me, and had been all along.

So while I cannot yet claim that I can do this and other things he has suggested often or that I have yet developed the kind of skill in piercing the veil that my teacher tells me are possible, I am now certain that, given time and my willingness, I will be able to journey in these parallel dimensions more often and with greater ease.

In this way, The Law of Dreaming, along with my practice of The Law of Humility and The Law of Time and Timelessness, will lead me deeper into the Great Mystery. Yes, the more I listen to my teacher, the more I am certain that I will come to verify the fact that Merlin has shared with me on many occasions, "The Great Mystery," he has said, "appears to be divided into a myriad of things, but, in truth, is always one and indivisible."

Notes on The Law of Dreaming

The noble leader schooled in inquiry and self-discovery knows that the distinction between reality and dreaming is arbitrary. There is an illusion that prevents many from moving beyond the limitations of physical time, space, and form — it is the illusion that logic, reason, and the five senses are the keys to reality. The conceits of time, reason, and the five senses are, however, the starting point for learning the lessons that are part of the human experience. The Law of Dreaming will then allow those who wish to discover that all is new and fresh, authentic, original, and filled with joy in each present moment. The noble leader can inspire and demonstrate ways those he leads can begin to pierce the veil, enter the other dimensions, and come to value their surrender to the Great Mystery.

Chapter Twenty - The Law of Communion

*"Faith is not knowledge of an object
but communion with it."*
–Nicolas Gomez Davila

Aderyn's Notes

My master and I sat for more than an hour this morning before Arthur's arrival, first in quiet reflection and then reviewing my transcriptions from the last few lessons. It has become one of the ways he ensures that I am accurately capturing the information he shares. It also gives him the chance to instruct me more deeply in the art of listening. For, in making suggestions and additions here and there on the parchments I have transcribed, he allows me to better understand the subtlety of his message and additional things that I would have missed.

It is another example of how blessed I am to be in his presence and how everything he shares with me, from the most ordinary description of a mundane task to the most elevated technique for reflection, from the mixing of various potions and brews to some of the more arcane practices he is now introducing me to, provides me with another opportunity to deepen my knowledge of the healing arts..

*I have to smile within myself at the memory of those times, early in my appren-
ticeship with him, when I took offense and offered resistance to many of his
instructions. Of course, I did not know then how great his mastery was or what a
true privilege it was that he had selected me to serve him. As I am reflecting on
this, I also realize that as my resistance has decreased, the depth of my learning
has increased, as has Merlin's willingness to communicate more of the wisdom he
possesses.*

*When I share this with him, he smiles and is just about to say more when young
Arthur appears. After a few moments of greeting, my master calls us into the
stillness in preparation for the next lesson. And, while it should not surprise me,
when he begins speaking, I realize that the subject of today's session is, in fact, a
continuation of the message he was sharing with me before my liege lord arrived.
It is also at this moment that he smiles at me, his eyes confirming the truth of my
observation.*

Merlin's Lesson

Before we begin exploring the Law of Communion, I want to take a little time
to explore any thoughts or questions that have arisen since our last session
on the Law of Dreaming. Aderyn, would you start?

Aderyn

My words are not sufficient to describe the many journeys you have encouraged, and I must admit that you have thankfully prodded me to take. For
when I reflect back on the lack of understanding or recognition I had of how
confined I was to what you call the Realm of the Five Senses. I am truly
amazed. I am embarrassed to admit how limited my understanding was of
all that life truly offers.

Just exploring the space between the breaths, for example, which was one of
the first lessons you shared with me, proved to be a gift of remarkable value.

And then to be reminded of how many of the experiences I had as a young child, when I let my imagination lead me, had actually allowed me entrance into timelessness and dreaming, and sometimes into the multiple worlds that many call fantasy, but were, at that time, very real and wonderful for me.

I could, and will, say much more, especially about some of the ceremonies you have invited me to join, especially during our last journey to the Southern Kingdoms, where the wizards and mystics had assembled. As you know, during these ceremonies, I drank some of the sacred brews and experienced dimensions and states of being that I can not even yet describe.

Merlin smiles.

And you, Arthur, what have you discovered?

Arthur

Last evening, as I was making note of some of the experiences of the day, I was aware that, like Aderyn, before you introduced me to various techniques of breathing and different ways of looking to see what you call between the worlds, I was living my life within very defined and what I was certain were solid boundaries. It was only when you encouraged me to slow my breathing and you introduced me to different ways of holding my head and softening my eyes, that I began to experience the spaces within and between the layers of the physical world. And while I have not yet mastered this way of seeing, I sometimes glimpse what appear to me to be veils that can be eased aside to disclose what you call alternate and parallel realities. And like Aderyn, some of these experiences are more possible when you give me herbs to chew or brews to drink.

And I must admit that at first I was afraid. I was afraid to let go and allow the experience. And as you know, on occasion, this caused me to struggle and lose the contents of my stomach. But with your help, I was able to learn to relax and allow what I had always thought were solid boundaries to dissolve. And time and space to vanish. And now, I am no longer afraid; I am only humbled by the scope of the Great Mystery and realize that I now look forward to all that I still have to learn and to explore. And for all of this and more, my teacher, I am deeply grateful.

Merlin smiles and nods again.

Thank you both for what you shared. And let us now continue this journey together on which we have more, much more to discover. So let us turn our attention to the Law of Communion. It is a law that can serve as a great support to all of humanity and is of special value to those who lead. So let us begin by remembering that all things issue from and are a part of the Great Mystery.

This understanding is reduced or enhanced as a result of a particular portion of this Law of Communion, which deals with what is called 'communication.' While not commonly understood, communication is a way of calling others to come into oneness.

So it is a sacred process. One also allows each of us to come into alignment with others through the exchange of words, symbols, signs, or gestures. And the effectiveness of this call depends largely on the skill and art of the one who issues the call.

So hold close this truth. As you become more adept at communication, you will advance the opportunity of calling those you lead into the experience of oneness, while those who remain less proficient will continue to retard and obstruct others and therefore miss the opportunity to empower those they serve. Hence, my advice to you is to take note of the fact that although words are valuable in this practice, they are only partial in their effectiveness.

One's energy, rhythm, gestures, the pauses between the words one uses, and, above all, the intention held in one's heart and mind when these words, gestures, and signs are expressed, all of these things significantly enhance one's ability to call those one leads to the next level of their empowerment, consciousness, and alignment with the Great Mystery.

So, be mindful of the commitment required and the attention that needs to be focused on becoming more masterful in the art of communication. For it is indeed one of the instruments through which the Natural Flow expresses itself as wholeness, harmony, integration, and communion.

In addition, if you wish to be a noble leader, you will be wise to remember to do your best to speak from a place of the highest consciousness accessible to you and always with the goal of unifying rather than dividing, of inspiring rather than attempting to motivate through manipulation, exaggeration, or the promise of reward, fear, or threat. Remember that energy is both neutral and enormously powerful, and how energy is used and the intention behind its expression in word and gesture can cause your communication to become either an instrument of good or of harm.

Remember also to speak slowly enough and to select your words carefully and with sufficient consciousness so that the images, emotions, and experiences they evoke will be positive and inspiring. And whenever possible, avoid speaking when held captive by negative emotions, for it will be these negative emotions, and not the words or gestures, that will be communicated most strongly.

Also, I invite you to always speak responsibly by owning the feelings, desires, and underlying objectives that lie within at the time of your speaking, rather than attempting to mask them with careful phrasing and falsely painted images. Speak always as an ambassador of truth, but with the admission that the truth you are advancing is, in all likelihood, only a temporary stopping place on the road to a greater and deeper understanding. I also encourage you to speak as if you are speaking intimately to one, even if you are speaking to many. And to speak as if the one to whom you are speaking is precious and without equal.

In this way, communication becomes the invitation to come into communion, into wholeness and alignment. And because it is such a potent force, it can and, unfortunately, is often abused. Hence, you are cautioned to treat the invitations you issue as sacred. For the call to communion through communication is an invitation that can awaken in others the desire for the greater good.

Let us pause here, and in this space, I invite you to call to mind a time when your communication was truly in alignment with the greater good and was successful in unifying and bringing harmony and peace to those you were speaking to. And once you have arrived at the image, mark it well within you. And you may want to take the thumb and forefinger of your right hand and squeeze that same spot on your left hand. This will be a way of anchoring this experience in your physical body, so that at any time in the future, you wish to recall it, it will be more accessible to you.

**Merlin closes his eyes and begins a slow and hypnotic chant as both Arthur and
Aderyn seeks to discover their individual experiences and to anchor them.**

**After a while, he opens his eyes and silently studies the faces of his young
charges. And then, when he is satisfied that both have been successful, he clears
his throat and begins speaking in a soft voice that invites both to open
their eyes.**

Communication, well used, can also inspire others to go beyond the obstacles and resistances that all who walk this path of life encounter. And this call to communion through communication can also remind even the most disheartened and distempered of the value of patience, the need to pause, reflect, regain perspective, and then to call on inner resources for guidance.

Through conscious communication, one can inspire a deeper commitment to balance, build more stable bridges of understanding, deeper compassion, express forgiveness and kindness, and, of special import, true appreciation for the myriad ways one can begin to touch into the scope, grandeur, preciousness, and awe of the Great Mystery.

This call to communion, to oneness and wholeness through communication in words, gestures, and signs, is only one means of delivering this invitation. The demonstration and practice of silence is another path that you are encouraged to utilize. It will invite those you serve into a greater connection to the Natural Flow and support them in experiencing their connection with harmony and beauty.

Reflection, prayer, chanting, and meditation are also ways that will allow you and those you lead to surrender more deeply to the Great Mystery. As well as your willingness and ability to demonstrate genuine gratitude, openness, receptivity, the courage to go beyond previous boundaries, and finally, the willingness to express wonder, celebrate, play, and share the fullness of love and grace with others.

My young companions, the Law of Communion is a true and immeasurable gift that you, Arthur, as a noble and conscious leader, and you, Aderyn, as a practitioner of the healing arts, can guide those whom you serve to appreciate the precious gift of life.

#####

Merlin's Assignment

Take time to consider the many different ways you can communicate with those you lead and identify which ways already work most effectively for you and in which circumstances. Also, reflect on those forms of communication that may not yet be your strengths. Identify what you can do to further develop these areas of your skill and how different forms of communication – word, gesture, tone, intent, etc. - can best be combined to truly call those you serve into oneness.

Arthur's Notes Recorded on His Parchment, Later in the Day

With each lesson, my gratitude to my teacher and the Great Mystery grows. In just a matter of months, Merlin has shared skills with me that I know will serve me during the length of my life. How fortunate I am to be able to walk this path in the company of this noble sage who is both my guide and my protector. How graced I am to be given this opportunity to gain this understanding of how I can better serve my people.

I am also becoming more aware that I have grown much during this time, and yet, strangely, I do not feel older. Instead, I somehow feel younger and more open to life. And yet I also feel stronger.

So I stand in awe of the path I am so privileged to be on now. But if I am honest, I must also admit that the further I go on this path, the more intimidated I become of the scope and importance of the responsibility I will one day inherit. And yet I also understand that while these laws Merlin has been communicating to me are not easy to practice, if I stay true to their practice, I will be better prepared to keep faith with my promise to serve others with nobility and grace.

Notes on The Law of Communion

The Law of Communion helps all of humanity, and especially those who lead, to remember that everything is part of the Great Mystery. An essential aspect of this law is what is called 'communication,' and is the invitation to come into oneness.

Communication is a powerful and neutral invitation that can be used by the leader for either great harm or great good. A noble leader is advised to always speak from a place of higher consciousness and with the objective of unifying rather than dividing. Treat the invitation to oneness as sacred and always issue it as a representative of the Great Mystery. The Law of Communion is a true and priceless gift that the noble leader can use to guide those he serves to celebrate the precious gift of life.

Chapter Twenty -One - The Law of Silence

*"In Silence, there is eloquence. Stop weaving
and see how the pattern improves."*
–Rumi

Aderyn's Notes

Summer has not yet completed its reign, and the fullness of Fall has not yet arrived. So it is, as my Master tells me, a time of transition. It is also the time of the rains, and so there are increasing traces of coolness and dampness in the air as I take in wood for the first fire of the season, wood that I have gathered, stacked, under the roof's eve along the back of the cottage since Spring.

This is another of the many lessons Merlin has shared with me. "Do not wait until you need wood," he often told me early in my time of service with him. "It will be too late then, and wood will still be wet and unseasoned, something you will regret all winter. You would also be wise to consider how many other things you can do in advance that will serve you when they are needed in life."

With my liege lord not due to arrive and my master still in his private quarters, there is plenty of time to heat the interior of the cottage and make things ready for their next conversation.

And, while I cannot be certain, I sense, from the way my master has been pausing as he reviews the notes that I have copied on parchment from the most recent lessons and asks for the earlier transcriptions as well for reference, and then sits quietly in reflection, that we might be approaching the end or, at least, a pause in this series of lessons with my liege lord Arthur.

Of course, I have been in service to Merlin long enough to know that attempting to predict what he will do next is no small task and is rarely accurate. Although he has been instructing me more of late in the art of learning to access my inner wisdom and to listen more closely to the clues and suggestions that I discover, I still know better than to advance an opinion on this matter too soon.

One thing I do, however, know is that whatever transpires will be as it should be and will ultimately serve my liege lord and me for our best and highest good. I am still holding this thought when young Arthur arrives, and my master emerges from his quarters, and preparations begin for the next lesson.

Merlin's Lesson

My Son, let us talk today about the fact that although the physical world is resplendent with the sound of the Natural Flow – a gift those among us who can hear and who stop to listen know to be precious. It is also easy for us to become distracted by the almost unlimited variety of sounds that issue from the world of man. These often, in fact, become so seductive that they cause many of us to forget the value and beauty of the silence that exists within and beyond the noise, and that we can access it within ourselves whenever we choose.

It is also true that as humanity increases in both its numbers and the diversity of its activities, the sound of the Natural Flow and of silence may well be further overwhelmed and may, for many, become much harder to hear than the sounds created by those of us who wear this human form.

208

Hence, if you wish to lead with nobility, I encourage you to practice listening to the sounds of the Natural Flow and to also enter into the silence as often as possible so that you may stay attuned to the Great Mystery. This will also help those you serve, for by witnessing you in this practice, they will be encouraged to do the same. Also, understand that learning to be in the silence is not a denial nor a condemnation of the remarkable variety of sounds that occur in the world of man, but it is an important way of staying attuned to the subtleties and the magic of the Natural Flow while it is still possible to hear.

Practicing this art of being in and with the silence will also enable you to better experience the benefits of the Law of Inquiry and Self-Discovery, and the Law of Humility. It will help you to learn how to differentiate between believing and knowing and to confront and befriend the doubts and fears, concerns, and conundrums that arise when you, as all of us who wear this form, become too immersed in physical reality.

To find the right balance in your life and come to know the difference between external engagement and internal reflection and observation is another gift that going into the silence will present. Also, remember that it will serve you greatly to make it a habit to seek the kind of counsel and guidance that can only be found through surrendering to the silence and, through it, to the Great Mystery.

When practicing the Law of Communion, if you make it your practice to pause only briefly in the silence before you speak on matters of consequence or before you attempt to make sense of the sounds of the world, you will be greatly advantaged. Yes, if you immerse yourself in silence in search of guidance before you act, great good will come to you and those you lead.

So the more you become comfortable in the silence and the more frequently you take up honored and sacred residence there, the more you will experience the gifts of refreshment, renewal, and nourishment that await all willing to enter the Great Mystery through this doorway.

In this way, you will be better able to find your way back when you step off the path, find the best way forward when the terrain is particularly difficult and arduous, and find your connection to truth when the turbulence of emotion and the illusions of the mind arise to obscure your discernment.

In the silence, My Son, you will most quickly sense when you are out of alignment and captured by disharmony and, as a result, be in a position to better part the veils of confusion and experience comprehension and right action. In the silence, you will glimpse the root of anger and bring the balm of patience, understanding, compassion, and forgiveness to the many thoughts, people, and events that may trigger reactions and distemper within you.

Silence is a sacred path. It will take you deeper, always deeper into the Great Mystery. And, when on this sacred path, you will come to better appreciate and celebrate the gift of your life and, in turn, be able to introduce those you serve to the true inner symphony of grace and wisdom that is available through this direct experience of the silence, which is the sacred nectar that nourishes the wise and the courageous.

So let us pause for a few moments for any comments or questions you may have. Or if there are none, let's take some time to have another direct experience of the silence.

When neither Arthur nor Aderyn seems inclined to speak, Merlin closes his eyes and begins a low chant that both his charges find impossible to resist.

#####

Merlin's Assignment

I invite you to find the place where sound and silence meet. Look also for the silence in the noise and the noise in the silence. And find the place where both can lead you deeper into the Great Mystery.

Arthur's Notes Recorded on His Parchment, Later in the Day

When I was younger and Merlin would talk to me about silence, I thought he meant the absence of sound. So, when he asked me to close my eyes and enter the stillness, I was always disappointed because what I experienced was an increase in the noise of the thoughts present in my mind. And the more I sought to quiet these thoughts, the louder and more uncontrollable they seemed to become. As a result, I was often discouraged and felt that I would never be worthy of this path my teacher was inviting me to walk on with him.

It was only as my time with Merlin continued that I came to understand that my mind would, on almost all occasions, continue to generate this fury of thoughts. For that, Merlin told me, is its job. But it is your job, he said, to choose when to give it latitude to do its job and, at the same time, when to be in silence and to direct my attention between my breaths, between the thoughts, between my feelings and between my other movements and actions Or perhaps it is more accurate to say that my job is to learn to move between the breaths, the thoughts, the feelings, and the sounds and into the silence.

Thanks to Merlin, I have also been able to discover that sometimes silence is very loud and all-encompassing, and it fills me with awe. Sometimes silence is soft, sweet, and nurturing, and I would do anything to remain within it. Sometimes it comes cloaked as a single sound, like the echo of a bell or the buzzing of bees in a field. Sometimes it appears as a pure form of emptiness, and sometimes as more fullness than I think I can contain. Sometimes, it is nothing that can be described. And so I now know that silence is many things and that it is different for each of us, each time we surrender to it.

Notes on The Law of Silence

Life is a precious symphony of sound to those able to hear and willing to listen. As the world of man increases in numbers and scope, it adds an incalculable range of notes from its activity to this symphony. So great is this sound of humanity's activity that it often obscures the sound of the Natural Flow. Learn to listen closely and find those places where the natural sound can still be heard. Learn to listen within the sacred vessel of silence for that renews, refreshes, and leads one deeper into the Great Mystery. Silence is the doorway through which the leader can walk to experience the sacred nectar of life, so he can share it with those he leads.

Chapter Twenty-Two - The Law of Leading From The Heart

*"When the heart speaks, the
mind finds it indecent to object."*
-Milan Kundera

Aderyn's Notes

*I hear my master rise before me and go out into the forest just as the first hints of
light are making their presence felt. While it is not unusual for him to be awake
at all hours of the day and the night, for some reason, I sense there is something
special about his early dawn departure. And just as I get the fire going and begin
to heat the water for our morning herbal brews, he returns carrying the limb of a
tree. It is a little longer than the height of an average man, is mostly straight, and
shows a vibrant color in those places where bark has come free. It appears to be a
rare find.*

*Leaning it against the wall to the left of the hearth and close to where he normally
sits during the indoor lessons, he turns and smiles and tells me that it is part of the
assignment he plans to give Arthur at the end of this session.*

He is about to turn away and enter his private quarters when he turns back and tells me that after our midday lesson is concluded, we will be pausing this series.

When I asked him if he thinks he will resume this series at a later time, and if I should therefore wait to incorporate all of the various notes onto a single roll of parchment, he considered my question for a moment or two. Then tells me that while he cannot be certain, he feels that this group of lessons, including the one he will share with Arthur at midday, will serve as a set unto themselves. He seems about to say more and then smiles, a sign that for him, the Great Mystery will be the ultimate decision-maker on this matter.

Merlin does not appear again until midday when Arthur arrives, and we are called into the silence in preparation for the next lesson.

Merlin's Lesson

My Son, although many advance the belief that the mind is the main center of intelligence and guidance for those of us who wear this human form, and while the mind is a most unique and valued ally, in the end, it is an instrument that functions best when it is at the disposal of a much greater and higher source of wisdom and intelligence, and that source speaks through the heart. And, this truth does not simply refer to the physical heart, that organ that enables life to pulse and flow continuously within us, but instead, it refers to the spiritual dimensions of the heart and the access it has to the Great Mystery. This is the center from which feeling, compassion, understanding, knowledge, harmony, wisdom, communion with the whole, and genuine wisdom come.

So, for one who seeks to lead with nobility and consciousness, there is no greater truth I can impart to you. The wisdom of the heart is the key to experiencing genuine feelings, which are among the most relevant and trusted allies you will ever have.

The heart is the doorway to the soul and, through it, to the Great Mystery. Hence, you are advised to never go faster than feeling can follow and always to stay in touch with and, first and finally, consult with the wisdom of the heart for all that you say and do.

The mind may be the repository of information. It may, at times, excel at evaluating and processing that information. It also serves as a source of reference and can be used to compare and contrast this with that. But, in the end, it is only as accurate and valid in these manipulations of information as is the validity of the information stored there, and that information and wisdom are accessed through the heart.

So if you truly wish to lead, always begin and end with your consultation with the heart. Only by leading with and from the heart will you ever truly represent the Great Mystery and act in concert with the Natural Flow. Only when you are in deep communion with that which is called love, awe, and compassion, only when you are capable of acknowledging your gratitude for the gift of your life, can you ever hope to serve the greater good.

Ideas, concepts, beliefs, theories, and the formulation of these into what are called systems and philosophies have ruled most of humanity for much of its history. Given enough time, most systems, concepts, and philosophies created by the mind generally prove themselves to be temporary and limited, while the wisdom of the heart, deeply experienced and expressed directly, has always been the shortest and most reliable path to an enduring form of truth.

So I invite you to pause and differentiate, as often as possible, between the wisdom of the heart and the thoughts, concepts, and beliefs that issue from your mind. Information that is, unfortunately, too often mistaken for wisdom in our time.

My son, you are also advised to always seek a direct experience of life.

Immerse yourself in the practices that are a part of each phase of life. Stay true to the journey of inquiry and self-discovery and observe and experience the lives, hopes, challenges, and dreams of those you serve. In this way, and only in this way, can you demonstrate the wisdom of the heart rather than fall victim to the call of emotions.

The wisdom of the heart is not selfish, nor is it driven by the desire for reward, or the need for recognition, approval, or acknowledgment. The wisdom of the heart does not separate or divide and does not advance the well-being of self over the well-being of another. It is not judgmental about the origin of a person, the nature of their beliefs and customs, or their status. These things are measured by most in our time on some arbitrary scale of relevance devised by man and not by The Great Mystery.

Indeed, the wisdom of the heart does not attempt to determine the worthiness of another, for it knows that all are part of the one. And, if you listen to the wisdom of the heart, you will not forget that leadership is an act of service and that it does not entitle you to accumulate large quantities of worldly possessions or expect special status or power over others as rewards for this service. And leadership is certainly not a position that entitles you to believe you are superior to others.

A noble leader knows or eventually comes to learn that the wisdom of the heart always calls him to demonstrate and advance the greater good, to wrap those he leads in the blanket of fairness and justice, and to ensure the appropriate and equal distribution of the natural resources that are true gifts from the Great Mystery to all.

So, my Son, if there is only one law you choose to practice, I encourage you to practice and master The Law of Leading From The Heart. Do so with genuine commitment and courage, and you will have access to the wisdom you will need to stay in tune with the Natural Flow and to be of genuine service to the Great Mystery.

For it has been written: Pursue a spiritual path (the path of the heart) with courage, and you will change who and what you are. Then there is no turning back. No regression, only forward movement to higher levels of consciousness.

Therefore, if you always practice this Law and share its message with those you lead, if you remind them that this law is the very reason and purpose you and they have taken on human form on this physical plane, you will be giving them a gift of inestimable value.

And so, my Son, your task and responsibility as a noble leader will always be to remind yourself and those you serve of this reason and purpose, and to inspire and support all whom you encounter in all ways to create a world in all of those you lead and their progeny more fully understand that they have both the right and the responsibility to identify, develop and share the unique and distinct gifts they have come here to this physical plane to share. For that, in the end, it is what they have come to this physical plane to do. And that is what everyone who is called to serve as a leader is called to aid them in remembering.

#####

Merlin's Assignment

After careful contemplation and observation, identify those instances in which your practice of The Law of Leading from The Heart allows you to be in alignment with the Great Mystery.

As a final assignment, I invite you to take this wood in hand, to live with it for a while until it speaks to you, and then, when you are moved, create a walking staff. While you are in that process of doing this, infuse it with the true spirit of The Law of Leading From The Heart so that whenever you hold it in your hand and feel its heft and its strength, you will be reminded of the path you can follow on the road to noble leadership and conscious governance.

Arthur's Notes Recorded on His Parchment, Later in the Day

At the end of our lesson on this day, as has been the case at the end of each of our previous lessons, it took Merlin a little while to "come back into himself' as he says. So I waited in the silence with Aderyn.

Finally, Merlin opened his eyes, stood, and called me to him. Before he spoke, I sensed that he was going to tell me this series of lessons was complete. Having had the honor of being in his company and under his protection and tutelage for a number of years, I have grown accustomed to reading some of his rhythms and the signs he gives before he translates them into words. As a result, I was not surprised to find that my sense was accurate.

However, I must admit that I still felt an immediate sadness that these sessions, which have contained so much valuable guidance on life, leadership, and governance, have come to an end. And yet, I also knew that I should acknowledge the sadness within me, but that I should not dwell on it, especially when Merlin had given me so very much in so many ways. How can I be sad when this man, whom I love so dearly and honor so deeply, and who has already taught me so much about my life, tells me it is now time for me to go deeper in search of my understanding and practice of these wise and valuable laws he has shared with me and that I can now practice and make my own forever?

How can I be anything but grateful that, at least for a while longer, I will still be blessed to be in Merlin's presence and be the recipient of the knowledge and wisdom that always flows from him like a fountain directly from the Great Mystery?

These are just some of the thoughts that were circling in my mind as he reached out and enfolded me in his warm and bearlike embrace. Then, when he stepped back, it seemed to me that, in addition to that sparkle that is so often in his eyes, there were hints of tears present that matched my own.

Oh, how I love and honor this extraordinary being without whom I would be so much the poorer.

Notes on *The Law of Leading From The Heart*

The mind is only an instrument at the disposal of a much greater and higher source of knowledge and wisdom centered in the heart. For the leader who seeks to lead with nobility and consciousness, there is no greater truth. The wisdom of the heart is the doorway to the soul and, through that, to the Great Mystery. The content stored in the mind is only as valid and accurate as the truth that comes from the heart. The wisdom of the heart is not selfish, exclusive, and is not directed by the need for reward, recognition, or acknowledgment. If the leader practices only one law, the Law of Leading From The Heart is key, for it contains all of the other laws.

Chapter Twenty-Three - Closing Remarks

"Be the change you want
to see in the world."
-Mahatma Gandhi

Dear Reader,

I have waited until you have had the opportunity to spend some quality time with Merlin's Laws before offering these closing comments. I have done this in the hope that I can now express my perspectives on what I sincerely believe is the value of the wisdom he shared with me and how it can, I believe, have a significant and constructive impact on the enormous travesty currently being perpetrated on our nation by individuals who call themselves Americans and have been elected to serve the greater good, but who have clearly lost both their integrity and their way.

In saying this, I do not wish to exacerbate the very significant divides that currently exist in our nation today. At the same time, however, having had the privilege of receiving and working with the information contained in the pages of this book, I would be remiss if I did not acknowledge that I believe our nation is currently facing the most egregious threat to our democracy and our way of life in our nation's 250 year history, and that Merlin's wisdom and that insights, that once shaped a future king and served as a vital guide to address some of the same loss of personal character and an abdication of the role of true leadership in his time, can now be used to defend and then strengthen democracy.

I know claims about dangerous threats have been made, at various times in our history, and most particularly during the Civil War and then the assassination of Abraham Lincoln - two events that constitute the last major assault on our nation by forces within our country.

I believe, however, that the current threat being advanced by Donald Trump and his blatantly unfit and incompetent administration, the ineffective and recalcitrant MAGA members in both houses of Congress, and the blatantly biased MAGA majority on the Supreme Court, together pose an unprecedented threat. Indeed, in addition to the impact this cabal is already having on our form of government and our way of life, if it succeeds in its now clear and current objectives, I believe it will put all of us as citizens, all of humanity, the other species, and our precious habitat at even greater risk from what is called The Sixth Extinction Event.

You see, climate change, with its growing catastrophes and what will soon be unprecedented climate migration, was not a concern during any of the previous threats to the well-being of our democracy and our way of life. However, if we have both the wit and courage to pay attention to the warnings from the majority of the world's scientists and experts, and capitalize on doing all that we can and is in our power in the very limited time we have to identify and implement possible solutions, we may be able mitigate some of the challenges and prepare for many of the consequences that may now be unavoidable. But if we fail to heed the warnings and do not do what can still be done, neither we nor our adversaries in this struggle will survive.

For these reasons, I believe this time calls out loudly and urgently, and the emergence of a new generation of strong, noble, conscious, and visionary leaders, leaders who have the capacity and competence as well as the courage, intelligence, integrity, and maturity to practice governance for the greater good of the greatest number. And, I most certainly believe that this time also calls out to We the People, who are citizens and members of the Fifth Estate in our system of checks and balances, to do all that we can to exercise all of our God-given, unalienable rights, freedoms and responsibilities - and most especially our right to utilize economic protest in the form of non-violent work slowdowns, general strikes, boycotts, and even temporary tax withholding revolts.

Yes, we are being called to use these rights to demand that our current government and its sycophants and enablers stop their assault on our Constitution, the Rule of Law, and our way of life, and return to doing the job of being our public servants and the employees elected to serve the will of We the People. And should this prove to be unacceptable to them, then it should be our goal to demand their resignations. For as is clearly and eloquently stated in our Declaration of Independence that launched this nation, "*it is the Right of the People to alter or to abolish it (this government) and to institute new Government, laying its foundations on such principles and organizing its powers in such a form, as to them shall seem most likely to effect their Safety and Happiness.*"

And when I speak of 'We the People,' there is another fundamental truth I believe we would be wise to keep in mind. There is no time for hesitation, equivocation, or procrastination. Instead, this is the time when we who are citizens of this democracy must pay heed to the guidance found in the words of Saint Augustine, who said. "*He who created us without our help will not save us without our consent.*"

Yes, it is a time for each of us to dig deep and respond with genuine integrity and courage and, in this way, act not only for ourselves and our children, but for those who will come after us and for those around the world for whom our democracy has always been a beacon of light and hope.

It is also time we once again commit to a more elevated form of consciousness, the kind shared by Merlin with Arthur that sits at the heart of this book. It is time to practice the kind of mature and informed kind of leadership and noble governance, Merlin advised us to practice.. Time we remember that it is the quality of our character, our compassion, commitment to truth, and ethical and moral fiber that is needed now if we are to defend our democracy from these sad and desperate souls who have fallen victim to a disease of the soul and virus of the mind, that our Algonquin, Cree, and Ojibwa brothers and sisters called "WETIKO," and the remarkable C.G. Jung called The Totalitarian Virus. Yes, it is time to stop colluding with these individuals who have lost their way, reclaim our sovereignty, and defeat their malevolent efforts. And then, having done this, it will be time to revisit, redefine, and strengthen our Constitutional Democracy to protect it from future malevolence.

Before closing, I invite all of us - Republicans, Democrats, Independents, Libertarians, as well as those who claim no political affiliation- to say enough to the chaos, inconsistency, incompetence, and the avalanche of hate and vengeance currently being advanced by this 2nd Trump Administration. I ask us all to say enough to the many restrictive and destructive things that are part of the reactionary and regressive philosophy that undergirds Project 2025. And to the limited beliefs and outmoded policies that are dark, rigid, and restrictive, that seek to drag us back in time to periods of repression, bigotry, suffering, and fear of the other. Yes, it is time to say enough to the unprecedented assault on and destruction of so much that we hold dear.

And so I hope you will hold close the values of character, as well as the wisdom of the heart, and the celebration of natural law and what Merlin called, The Great Mystery. I also hope you will take a little time to read our Declaration of Independence, our US Constitution, and our Bill of Rights. Read them slowly and allow these documents to remind you of what is truly at stake, and not just for those of us who are citizens and residents of this nation, but for people everywhere who long to live the lives and dreams they, too, were born to live. To honor the rights and privileges of all of humanity, regardless of race, creed, color, religious or spiritual persuasion, or political beliefs, and to return to being stewards of our earth in the tradition of past Wisdom

Keepers who served this miraculous and endangered habitat for hundreds of thousands of years.

And if you are also inclined, I ask you to consider adopting some of the additional suggestions I have included in another of my new books, *We the People - Democracy's Best and Last Hope.* It identifies 21 keys and cures that I believe can be highly effective in defending our democracy against tyranny.

Most of all, I invite you to re-read the last of Merlin's laws, the Law of Leading From The Heart. As Merlin shared, if there is only one law you ever practice, the wisdom of your heart will never let you down.

And I leave you with these lyrics that I wrote for one of the songs in my new concept album on Democracy. These words came to me as part of a download of poems and lyrics that came to me in February 2024, when I was hospitalized for an undiagnosed infection that had turned into a sepsis condition and almost cost me my life.

I Dreamed

I dreamed that I awoke one day
And all the world was new
The divisions, the delusions, and
Confusions spread by a madman
And a malicious few
No longer blocked the sun
Or prevented anyone
From receiving their due
And joy and friendship echoed
All across the land
And humanity
was finally able to get back
to its intended plan

For the next stage of revolution
Faster than evolution.

And in the heavens
The angels were singing
And on this fragile plane
The bells of freedom
And truth were ringing.

I know it is only a dream
My friends
But among the secrets in my heart
Is the knowledge that this
Can be our reality
If we can come together
Follow our hearts
And do our parts

I dreamed that I awoke one day
And all the world was new
Divisions and delusions and
The malevolence of the few
No longer blocked the sun
And everyone upon the earth
Received their due.

I also close these words from American Poet, Archibald MacLeish, that I repeat often.

"There are those who say that the liberation
of humanity, the freedom of man
and mind, is only a dream.
They are right!

It is the American Dream."

In the spirit of collaboration and our mutual quest for a more perfect union

George Cappannelli

Santa Fe, New Mexico

August 15, 2025

Chapter Twenty-Four - About The Author

George Cappannelli is an award-winning author, film and television director, and sculptor. He has also served as a consultant and coach to a number of Fortune 500 companies, government agencies, and national associations, and has provided strategic coaching and innovative research in 3 Presidential Campaigns, a US Senate Campaign, and a local Mayoral Campaign.

He and his wife, Sedena, are Co-Founders of AgeNation, a multi-platform media company dedicated to redefining what it means to live consciously and age wisely in the 21st Century. and are also Co-Founders of Empower New Mexico, a 501C3 non-profit that serves the needs of vulnerable elders.

George is a leading expert on individual, organizational, and societal change and has extensive experience in both the public and private sectors. Under the banner of The Information and Training Company his clients include Fortune 500 companies, government agencies and national associations: Accenture, The Boeing Company, Hughes Space & Communications, TRW, PepsiCo, NASA, Taco Bell, Pacific Bell, Sun MicroSystems, Honeywell, National Oceanographic Aeronautics Administration (NOAA), Oracle, Space Systems/Loral, The National Forest Service, Grumman, The U.S. Navy, The U.S. Postal Service, The Walt Disney Company, The Israel Government, The Los Angeles Times, and many others.

In addition to his work in the corporate sector and his work on conscious living and wise aging under the auspices of AgeNation, he has had a very diverse career. He has been privileged to work on projects with world leaders, including Desmond Tutu, Lech Walesa, Golda Meir, Mother Teresa, and the Dalai Lama. As President and Founder of two New York film and television production companies, Theater Visions and Axial Productions, his work has been recognized with several International Film Awards, as well as ANDY, CLEO, two special category EMMY Awards, and two Telly Awards.

He served as Executive Director of The Sedona Institute and as one of the Directors of The Society for the Advancement of Human Spirit, an organization chaired by The Dalai Lama.

He served as a lead facilitator for Insight Seminars and was a member of the group that founded The Insight Consulting Group. His background also includes work in the advertising and marketing field, where he served as Executive Vice President and Creative Director of Allerton, Berman and Dean, A New York firm.

In 1991, he returned to the political arena, where he managed the launch of Jerry Brown's U.S. Senate Campaign in California. He also served as a special consultant in the 1992, 2000, and 2008 Presidential Campaigns and in 2004 served as the chief strategist in a mayoral campaign that elected the first democrat in 30 years by the largest plurality in the town's history.

Mr. Cappannelli is a well-known keynote speaker. His award-winning sculptures in stone, wood, and bronze are in public and private collections. As a writer, he is the co-author with his wife, Sedena, of 5 books: "Say Yes to Change," "Authenticity, Do Not Go Quietly, The Best Is Yet To Be, and Getting Unstuck, and their new book Making The Best of The Rest of Your Life. (Due out soon.) He is also the author of We the People, Democracy's Best and Last Hope, Conversations with Merlin, It's About Time and Timelessness, A Man Is..., and a trilogy of novels entitled "Old Stones & Promises", and a new novel, "Life After Life After..."

George is an Emmy Award-winning producer/director. His innovative Theater Visions Series brought plays from Broadway and Off-Broadway to television, as did his Inside Music Series. More recently, he co-produced and directed the Award-Winning, 40 Episode Ageless Living PBS Television Series, which originally aired nationally on PBS and is now available on Amazon Prime and Tubi, and Touching The Heart and Healing The Soul, the Telly Award-winning Live Stream 2021 Pre-inaugural Special.

Chapter Twenty-Five - Other Books In Print

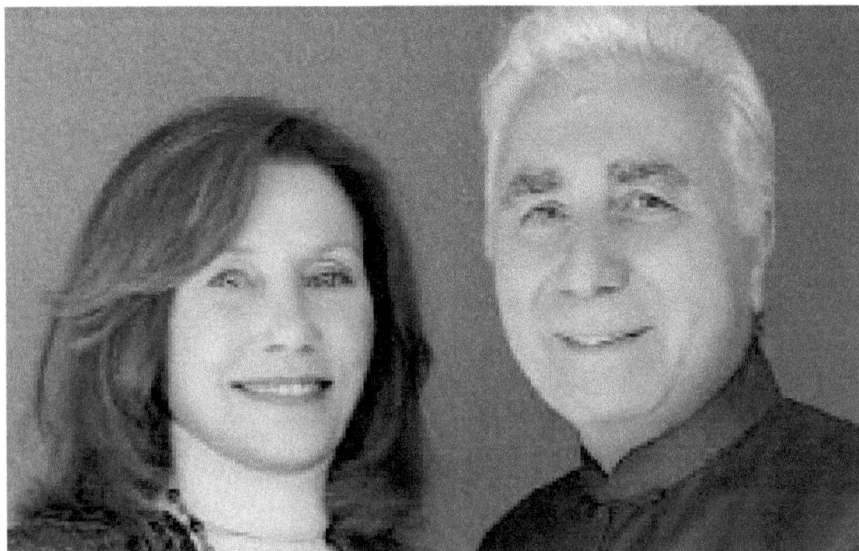

Other Books In Print By George & Sedena Cappannelli

Do Not Go Quietly, A Guide To Living Consciously and Aging Wisely For

People Who Weren't Born Yesterday - 2013 Hardcover – Winner of 9 National Book Awards, including the Gold Nautilus Award – Originally published by Hay House/AgeNation/Agapi Media.

Hardcover is now available through the authors

Paperback – Available from Beaufort Books –

Kindle Version on Amazon

By George & Sedena Cappannelli

The Best Is Yet To Be, How To Live Wisely and Fall In Love With Your Life AGAIN 2014

Hardcover – Simple Truths Publisher –

By George & Sedena Cappannelli

Getting Unstuck – 10 Simple Secrets To Embracing Change and Celebrating Your Life - 2015

Hardcover – Simple Truths – Volume Group Discounts Available

Authenticity: A Guide To Greater Meaning and Purpose At Work & Home - 2007

Originally Published by Emmis Books – Paperback –

By George & Sedena Cappannelli

Say Yes To Change, 25 Keys To Winning In Time of Transition - 2004

Paperback – Originally Published By Walking Stick Books –

By George & Sedena Cappannelli

By George Cappannelli

I Dream of A New America, Keys To Reclaiming The Heart and Soul of America - 2008

Originally Published – Bridger Press – Paperback

By George Cappannelli

It's About Time – How to make time your ally and life your game - 2005
Onlife Publishers - Paperback
By George Cappannelli

We the People - Democracy's Best and Last Hope - 2025
Onlife Publishing - Paperback and Kindle editions

DVDs By Sedena Cappannelli

PEP – Personal Energy Program - 2009
DVD – By Sedena Cappannelli

Chapter 26

"We shall not cease from exploration
  And the end of all of our exploring
  Will be to arrive where we started
  And know the place for the first time."
  -T.S. Eliot